TURN THIS BOOK INTO A
BEEHIVE!

And 19 Other Experiments and Activities That Explore the Amazing World of Bees

by Lynn Brunelle · illustrated by Anna-Maria Jung

WORKMAN PUBLISHING
NEW YORK

For Keith, Kai, and Leo. You're the bee's knees.

Copyright © 2018 by Lynn Brunelle

Illustrations by Anna-Maria Jung

Library of Congress Cataloging-in-Publication Data is available.

ISBN 978-1-5235-0141-0

Editor: Justin Krasner
Art Director: Colleen AF Venable
Designer: Carolyn Bahar
Production Editor: Amanda Hong
Production Manager: Doug Wolff

Workman books are available at special discounts when purchased in bulk for premiums and sales promotions as well as for fund-raising or educational use. Special editions or book excerpts can also be created to specification. For details, contact the Special Sales Director at the address below, or send an email to specialmarkets@workman.com.

Workman Publishing Co., Inc.
225 Varick Street
New York, NY 10014
workman.com

WORKMAN is a registered trademark of Workman Publishing Co., Inc.

Printed in China
First printing April 2018

10 9 8 7 6 5 4 3 2 1

CONTENTS

HELP THE BEES HELP THE WORLD

Bees. The very mention of these fuzzy insects may make you have a hankering for honey or start swatting the air. But whether you love 'em or hate 'em, we need bees for our survival.

That may sound melodramatic but it's true.

Bees are a keystone species. That means that plants and animals in an ecosystem depend on them for survival. If a keystone species is removed, the whole ecosystem crumbles.

We depend on bees to pollinate the plants that give us food. Some examples are almonds, squash, cucumbers, apples, oranges, blueberries, and peaches. One out of every three bites you take comes to you courtesy of a bee.

Bee-pocalypse

We've relied on the honeybee to pollinate our food plants for centuries, but lately there's been a big problem. In the past few years, honeybee colonies have begun collapsing. Every morning, all over the world, billions of bees leave their nests for a busy day of gathering nectar and spreading pollen from plant to plant. Strangely, many aren't returning home. In the United States alone, there is an annual loss of 30 percent of honeybee colonies.

What's Causing It?

Scientists can't boil it down to only one thing. Insecticides, diseases, pollution, and loss of habitat all factor into the rapid decline of bees. Farmers use insecticides to keep pests from eating and ruining crops. The chemicals they use are specific to certain insects, but they may damage a bee's memory and prevent it from finding flowers to pollinate and other bees to mate with. Habitat and climate change can affect flower blossoming times, which can mess up the foraging habits of a bee. And there are other factors such as viruses, fungi, or mites that infest nests and spread disease. In addition, beekeepers have extended the pollination seasons, giving bees less time to recover.

Most likely the decline is a combination of these things. The important thing to know is that it is happening and that if it continues like this, it won't be long before we have empty gardens, orchards, and dinner plates.

No bees means no pollination, no plants, no us.

It's a problem we need to fix. Here's the upside: You can help make a difference.

Bee the Change!

Whatever is causing the decline, it doesn't have to be a one-way street to disaster. There are things we can do to reverse the damage.

It doesn't take much. You don't need any fancy equipment or protective gear. In fact, you hold a solution right in your hands. This book is chock-full of information and activities that will help you understand these amazing insects. But it's not just the bee-all and end-all on bees . . .

This book can actually be turned into a home for some amazing pollinators—mason bees.

So, what are mason bees? And how are they different from honeybees? First, they don't sting (unless you squeeze them). Second, they don't make

YOU BEE THE CHANGE!

honey. Third, they are amazing at pollinating plants. In fact, they're pollinator superheroes! A single mason bee can pollinate as many flowers in one day as it takes 100 honeybees to do.

 =

Invite Bees to Your Place

There are about 150 different types of mason bees in North America. Chances are, no matter where you live, you probably have these helpful bees flying around. If you invite them into your yard, garden, rooftop, or fire escape, you're helping to solve the problem. Even a friendly flowerpot can provide a habitat. They're easy to please. Just make them feel welcome by providing a home, food in the form of lots of plants, water, and a clean, nontoxic space. In return you'll get happier plants, more fruits and vege-tables, and a healthier world.

This one small thing can make a big difference. And the power is at your finger-tips. You can turn *this book* into an inviting home for wild mason bees (see page 50 for instructions) and start changing the world today. But first, you'll need to learn more about bees!

What's the difference between a nest and a hive? When humans provide the nest, it's called a hive.

CHAPTER I

BEE SMART

There's more to bees than buzzing, stinging, and making honey. That barely scratches the surface of how amazing these creatures are. Bees are insect superstars! They're built for survival and their skills and talents help keep our lives sweet.

What Is a Bee?

Bees are pollinators. They fly from blossom to blossom in search of pollen and nectar. A flower's nectar is deep inside the flower. When bees land inside, they brush up against the parts of the flower that produce pollen. Pollen is sticky and it covers and clings to the bee's body as the bee slurps the nectar up with its long tongue.

When the bee lands on another flower, some of the pollen from the previous flower falls off, fertilizing the new flower. This process keeps plants reproducing.

While bees have stingers, they don't use them for hunting because they don't eat meat. Most bees only sting as a last resort if they feel threatened. Some bees don't sting at all.

Bees live on every continent except Antarctica and can be found in any environment that has flowers. There are more than 4,000 different kinds of bees in North America.

Bee Social or Bee Solitary

There are at least 25,000 different species of bees buzzing around the earth today. They can be divided up into two major groups—social bees and solitary bees.

Social Bees

Honeybees and bumblebees are social bees. They live as a colony in one nest, work together, and answer to one queen. The queen is the only bee laying eggs. Every other bee in the colony is working hard to take care of the queen and her babies by collecting nectar, producing honey, and protecting the nest.

HONEYBEES produce honey from the pollen and nectar of the plants they pollinate. In the wild they often build their nests in trees or rock crevices, but they will occasionally make themselves at home in attics or chimneys. Their nests are made out of wax formed into sheets of honeycomb. Depending on where they build, their nests can look either long and narrow (inside trees) or flat and wide (in chimneys or attics). They store their honey in honeycombs to feed their young in colder months. Unlike bumblebees and solitary bees, honeybees can live for multiple years, so they need to prepare and store food to survive through the winter. Most of the honeybees in the United States live in hives created by beekeepers. Because their stingers are barbed and attached to their abdomens, they can only sting once; the stinger then rips away, leaving the bee to die.

BUMBLEBEES have extremely fuzzy, round bodies. They are wonderful pollinators and very helpful for the garden. Bumblebees often nest in the ground but can be found above ground around patio areas or decks. They build their homes in shaded areas, under sheds or even in clumps of grasses. Their nests can look like piles of leafy rubble. Each spring, a queen will start her own new colony. She will only live for a year. If threatened, bumblebees will buzz loudly and may even chase invaders for a considerable distance and deliver painful stings. Unlike honeybees, bumblebees can sting more than once.

Solitary Bees

The other kind of bee is the solitary bee. Over 90 percent of bee species are solitary bees. These bees live on their own. They don't build colonies, have a separate queen, or have specific roles. Every female finds her own nest, lays her own eggs, collects her own pollen and nectar, and feeds her own offspring. However, despite working on their own, solitary bees often like to gather and live near each other. They do not produce honey, but they are some of nature's most amazing architects and most accomplished pollinators.

MASON BEES are the most common solitary bees in the United States. You can find about 150 different mason bee species buzzing, pollinating, and making homes all over North America. They're sometimes called orchard mason bees because they do so much to pollinate apple, cherry, and almond tree orchards. They find existing tunnels created by other insects to nest in and then use mud to seal off their egg chambers.

LEAFCUTTER BEES frequent meadows or gardens with leaves that are succulent and delicate. They seal their egg chambers with pieces of leaves.

CARPENTER BEES are found in humid areas with lots of lush blooms. They drill holes into soft wood to make their nesting tunnels.

DIGGER BEES are found in dry areas and around plants. They often dig into the soft, sandy soil of cliffs to make their nests.

MINING BEES can be found in meadows, lawns, and orchards with plenty of flowering trees. They dig narrow channels underground or in sandy cliff sides.

The Big and the Small World of Bees

There are over 25,000 species of bees buzzing around our planet. The smallest bee is the *Perdita minima*, found in the deserts of the United States. It's the size of a sesame seed. The largest is the *Bombus dahlbomii*, or giant bumblebee, from South America. It can grow as big as 1½ inches (3.8 cm) long. That's the size of your thumb!

Bees' Nests

Mason Bee

Bumblebee

Honeybee

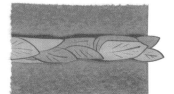

Leafcutter Bee

Carpenter Bee

Mining & Digger Bees

Bees in History

The ancestors of bees, flies, and wasps appeared on the planet about 300 million years ago. About 100 million years ago, bees branched off from the family tree.

Before that time, plants depended mostly on the wind to carry pollen from one flower to another. That process was slow and challenging. Luckily, bees showed up and preferred eating pollen instead of other insects. They began bringing pollen from one plant to another and another and another. Flowering plants thrived. New species developed. Wild and wonderful new

blossoms, colors, aromas, and shapes began to appear, all thanks to a bunch of busy and hungry bees.

The earliest bees were solitary bees. Each female built her own nest, foraged for food, and laid eggs. Over time, some bees evolved to live together in social groups. They worked together to make nests in crevices, in trees, or in the ground. They shared and stored food, cared for their babies, and defended their territory. These bees were the first honeybees. The food they stored in their nests was honey.

Fast-forward to about 9,000 years ago. Early humans discovered that some bee nests held a sweet delight and they were hooked. It was the beginning of a beautiful and long relationship between people and bees. Paintings of bees have been discovered in prehistoric caves. Scenes of beekeeping are painted on the walls of ancient tombs. Drawings and carvings of bees show up in ancient Egyptian hieroglyphics. Egyptians even buried honey with their pharaohs. (Honey has a heck of a shelf life too. When archaeologists excavated a 3,000-year-old tomb, they discovered honey that was still edible!) Bees appear on ancient Roman coins, on ancient Greek pottery, in medieval European illuminated manuscripts, and in timeless folktales from around the world.

But it isn't just the sweetness of honey that people cherished. They were aware of the link between bees and healthy crops. As humans began developing agriculture, they took bees along to help with pollination.

Egyptian Hieroglyphics

Cave Drawings

Greek Pottery

Is That a Bee?

Some wasps and flies often get mistaken for bees because they share those familiar yellow-and-black stripes or general body type. Wasps are distant cousins, and some flies have simply evolved to look like bees. But while they may look alike, they don't act alike, and they sure don't eat the same things. Here's the buzz on a few insects that are not bees.

Wasps Aren't All Bad

There are over 30,000 different species of wasps. Wasps, like bees, can be solitary or social. And most are stingless and helpful. They gobble up harmful bugs that threaten crops and people.

Wasps

Wasps have hairless, skinny-waisted bodies with long, dangly legs. They might sip at a flower or two, but they're hunters. (Wasps are the ones that land on your sandwich at a picnic and start gnawing away at your ham and cheese.) Wasps hunt other insects and drag them back to their nests to feed on. Many also sting. They're designed with powerful, venom-packed stingers that they use to disable their prey and to protect themselves. Some wasps aren't afraid to zap anything that gets in their way, including you, so watch out! Here are a few to avoid:

COMMON TYPES OF WASPS

PAPER WASPS are brownish in color with yellow or reddish markings. They live in colonies and get their name from the paperlike material of which they construct their nests. These nests are often umbrella-like in shape and are found hanging from twigs and branches, under eaves and porch ceilings, or in the attic. Paper wasps eat other insects including caterpillars and flies. While not usually aggressive, they can deliver a painful sting if threatened.

YELLOWJACKETS have a yellow-and-black color pattern and are about the length of your thumbnail. They build papery, basketball-size nests out of chewed-up plant fiber, which hold colonies of up to 4,000 insects. The nests can be in trees, bushes, or attics. Some are underground. Aside from their diet of bugs, these insects are picnic pests, as they love sweets and meats. They're also very territorial and will sting repeatedly if they feel threatened.

MUD DAUBERS are long and slender and usually black in color, and they may have pale markings or a metallic luster. They do not live in colonies but make individual homes out of mud. They rarely sting, and help control spiders.

BALD-FACED HORNETS are largely black in color, with a mostly white face. They live in paper nests usually built in late summer that contain between 100 and 400 members. They can sting repeatedly and are much more aggressive than other species, so stay back!

Flies

There are more than 100,000 species of flies on the planet. There are tiny fruit flies that live near ripe fruit. There are annoying house flies that buzz and avoid capture. There are biting horseflies and deerflies. Flies can live pretty much anywhere and mostly eat dead stuff. Some flies also like flowers. They can be found in garbage piles, pet areas, barns, and dumpsters. They don't have stingers, but they can bite.

Rule of Thumb

In general, though there are exceptions, if you see a striped insect on a flower, chances are it's a bee. If you see one chewing on a salami sandwich, it's probably a wasp. And if it lands on garbage or your little brother's diaper, it's most likely a fly.

Who Brings the Sting?

Life as a small insect isn't always easy. There are predators to watch out for and a family to protect. For bees and similar insects, the sting's the thing. Bright colors and contrasting patterns say DANGER in nature. The yellow and black stripes of a bee are advertising a warning: Back off! Predators learn that the color and pattern can be associated with a nasty sting and keep away. Not all bees will sting, but when you see stripes, move slowly and steer clear. Most won't go out of their way to sting you, but if they think you are a threat, watch out!

Girl Power

Only female bees sting. Their stinger also doubles as an egg-laying structure, called an *ovipositor*.

What to Do If You Get Stung

Even with the best intentions, you just may threaten a bee or other stinging insect and before you know it, OUCH! Now what?

1. **Tell someone.** Some people are allergic to insect stings and need medical attention immediately. If you see hives (red bumps on your skin that sting or itch), feel like throwing up, are dizzy, or are having a hard time breathing, you could be allergic.

2. **Remove the stinger.** Many bees, wasps, and hornets have smooth stingers, but others have barbed stingers that hook into your skin and stay there when the insect flies away. Because the stinger still has venom in it, you need to get it out as soon as possible. Just don't pinch! You could squish more venom into the sting. Instead, scrape it out with the straight edge of something like a credit card.

3. **Wash with soap and water.** This gets rid of dirt, extra venom, or anything that might cause an infection.

4. **Ice the area.** The cold from the ice can keep swelling down. It can also numb the sting a bit so it doesn't hurt as much.

5. **Calm the sting.** Stings can feel *really* painful. You can mix baking soda and water to make a paste and spread it over the sting. This helps pull out the venom and calm the pain.

911

Call 911 if you or a person who has been stung has any of the following symptoms:
- Hives, itching, and flushed or pale skin
- Difficulty breathing
- Swelling of the throat and tongue
- A weak, rapid pulse
- Nausea, vomiting, or diarrhea
- Dizziness or fainting
- Loss of consciousness

CHAPTER 2

THE ABC'S OF BEES

Over time bees have evolved to become perfectly adapted for their lives as food gatherers. Their wings, eyes, fuzzy bodies, antennae, and more help them recognize and locate flowers, collect pollen and nectar, and navigate their way home.

Bee Anatomy

What makes a bee a bee? All bees are insects, which means they have three main body parts: a head, a thorax, and an abdomen. They also have six legs, two antennae, two pairs of wings, and a stinger if they're female.

· · · · HEAD · · · · · ·

· · · · THORAX · · · · ·

· · · ABDOMEN · · · ·

HONEYBEE

MASON BEE

Chow Hounds

Bees are built to find food. They have strong flying muscles, sharp eyesight, tasting antennae and toes, a sensitive sense of smell, and a downright shocking sense of touch. They're amazingly well equipped for bringing food back to their nests as well. Bees aren't just fuzzy for show; the tiny hairs that cover their bellies, backs, and chests collect pollen from the flowers they visit. Different bees have different ways of carrying pollen. Honeybees and bumblebees have little pollen "baskets" on their hind legs where pollen is stored. Mason bees stuff pollen around the hairs on their bellies. Other bees have ridges, spines, and brushes on their bodies for holding on to pollen.

How Does a Bee Fly?

To get from one blossom to another, a bee needs to fly. Crawling and climbing would take too much time and energy. But how do these insects lift themselves with their relatively tiny wings? The secret is in the movement and flow of air. Bees don't fly or glide like airplanes or birds. Instead, their wings move like fast and awkward helicopter blades. Bees fly an average of 15 miles per hour and their wings flap at 200 beats per second. The wings push air down, lifting the body up. At the bottom of each flap, the wings flip over and the angle creates more push downward to keep the bee in the air.

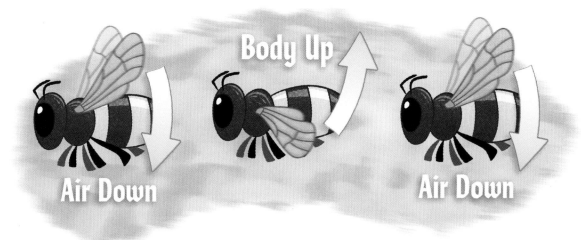

Bees like the bumblebee have chunky bodies because they need the muscle mass to keep flapping. The muscles that move the wings aren't attached to the wings. Instead, they're inside the thorax. The bee squeezes and flexes the muscles and the thorax changes shape, moving the wings up and down as they go. Tiny muscles that reach from the thorax to the wings are used for twisting the wings to change the angle.

EXPERIMENT:
Winging It

How is it possible for bees to stay in the air?
This experiment can show you how.

WHAT YOU NEED

- Your hand
- Water—in a large bucket, bathtub, pool, lake, pond, or the ocean

WHAT YOU DO

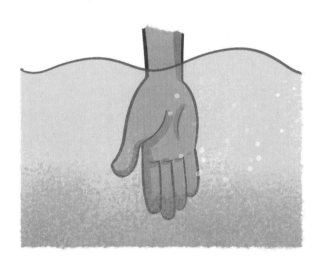

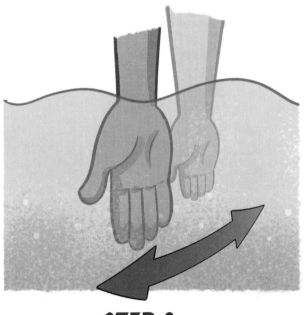

STEP 1:

Put your hand in the water, keeping your hand flat and fingers pointed down.

STEP 2:

Move your hand, front to back, in long, smooth strokes with your palm flat like a paddle. This is similar to how a bird flies.

TURN THIS BOOK INTO A BEEHIVE!

STEP 3:

Now try lots of short strokes. Does it feel different?

STEP 4:

Now move your hand in a figure-eight motion. Twist your hand so that the palm is always facing the direction of the push. What do you notice?

WHAT'S GOING ON?

The flow of water around your hand is similar to the flow of air around a bee's wing. When you move your hand in long, sweeping strokes like a bird flying, you can feel the water pushing your hand back and giving it a little lift. When you use short strokes in a figure-eight motion—the way a bee beats its wings—you get extra lift. You can really feel it just as your hand changes direction. There's more pressure and more lift. A bee has to beat its wings all the time. If it didn't, it would drop like a stone.

What Does a Bee See?

Bees have supersight. Unlike humans who have only one lens per eye, bees have a compound eye on each side of their head made up of over 5,000 individual lens parts called *ommatidia*.

Each ommatidium is like a different eye that points in a slightly different direction. It sends information back to the bee brain, where it is formed into a bigger picture like a pixel in a larger image. This allows bees to detect motion, light, and color.

And because they have eyes on the sides of their heads rather than on the front, bees have superpower depth and distance perception and an almost 360-degree view. They also have three small individual eyes at the tops of their heads that help them orient their position in space.

Bees can see things we can't. For example, air molecules scatter the light in the sky and create patterns invisible to the human eye. Bees see these patterns and use them like GPS to find their way home. Bees have the ability to see much faster than we do too. They have a higher "flicker" threshold, which means they can see things like individual flowers even as they are zipping over a landscape.

The world is colored differently for a bee. Humans can see a rainbow of colors on the spectrum from red, orange, yellow, green, and blue to violet. But bees can't see reds or oranges. Instead, they see colors closer to the violet and ultraviolet end of the spectrum, colors that are invisible to the human eye. Flowers that may appear plain to us may have lovely, bright ultraviolet patterns that are inviting to bees. They act as landing strips, signaling hungry bees and making finding nectar a lot easier.

Bee Scene

It's very rare, but sometimes people can see ultraviolet light. Injury or surgery can change how the eye sees and allow it to pick up more whitish-blue or whitish-violet color. The French painter Claude Monet had this condition after cataract surgery. Before the surgery he could see reds and oranges, but after surgery his range included more deep blues and purples.

When it comes to flowers and bees, there's more than meets the eye. What looks like a simple flower to us might be offering bees an ultraviolet light show.

EXPERIMENT:
Shape Up!

DISCLAIMER: This experiment takes about a week of observation and lots of patience.

How do bees know where and how to find good feeding spots? And how do they store away that knowledge and remember it from day to day? Here's an experiment you can do to see what a bee sees and what it remembers.

WHAT YOU NEED

- Adult to help out
- 1 cup (250 mL) water
- Saucepan
- ½ cup (110 g) sugar
- Three 3-inch-by-5-inch (76.2 by 127 mm) index cards
- Black marker
- A piece of tape (optional)
- Three sandwich-size ziplock bags
- Three small dishes or jar lids

WHAT YOU DO

STEP 1:

Make your homemade nectar.

(Real nectar, from flowers, is a similar sugary liquid.)

- Put the water in the pan and place it on a stove. Heat the water until it's about to boil. You will see tiny bubbles forming on the bottom of the pan.

- Stir in the sugar until it's dissolved.

- Let it cool completely.

STEP 2:

Set up the cards.

- On the first card, draw a triangle. On the second card, draw a circle. On the third card, draw a square. Make each shape big enough to cover most of the card and color in the shape so that it's solid black.

- Place each card into a separate ziplock bag and seal it so it will be protected from the weather.

- Take everything outside and place the cards face up in a flat sunny spot 2 to 3 feet (0.6 to 0.9 m) away from each other.

STEP 3:

Set up the dishes.

- Pour your homemade nectar into one of the small dishes. Fill the other two dishes with plain water. Make sure the level of the liquid is the same in each dish.

- Make a mark on the dish with the sugar water, using either your black marker or a small piece of tape.

- Place a dish next to each of the bags so that the shape can be easily seen. (You may want to tack down the bags with rocks so they won't move around if it gets windy.)

TURN THIS BOOK INTO A BEEHIVE!

STEP 4:
Observe.

- Set up a chair or a blanket nearby to keep watch for a while.

- What kinds of insects come by your "flowers"? How many days does it take before bees find the one with homemade nectar?

STEP 5:
Switch it up.

- A few days after you've seen bees at the homemade nectar dish, switch the cards so that the shape that was next to the homemade nectar is now by a dish of plain water.

- What happens in the next few days? Do the bees fly right to the sugar water? Do they fly right to the dish next to the shape that used to be by the sugar water?

- Leave the bags with the shapes where they are, but now move the sugar water dish to another shape that used to be next to a dish with plain water. What do you notice?

STEP 6:
Take it further.

- Try the experiment using different colors instead of different shapes. Make them all circles or triangles. Is there a difference? Are some colors more effective than others? Or try drawing faces. What do you notice?

WHAT'S GOING ON?

Your bees should be able to figure out which shape is near the homemade nectar. When you mixed up the shapes, did your bees follow the sugar or the shape?

    Bees make their way around the world using two things. First, bees use the sun as a compass. They remember the direction and location of things (their hive or nest, delicious nectar-filled flowers, your homemade nectar dish) in relation to the sun. And because they can see polarized light, unlike humans, bees can determine the direction from which sunlight is coming even in cloudy weather. Second, just like bees can see ultraviolet light in elaborate patterns on flowers, they can see manmade patterns as well. Bees recognize and memorize these patterns to remember where good feeding grounds are. Beekeepers who take care of many hives sometimes help their bees find their way home by putting a specific design on each hive. The bees see the design and recognize the pattern to remember which hive is theirs.

What Does a Bee Smell?

A bee's sense of smell is amazing. Mid-flight, they can use their antennae, mouths, and even feet to detect and locate scents from miles away. Special hairs on their legs and antennae can sense sweetness and saltiness, so all a bee has to do is hover over a flower to smell its sweet nectar or over a body of water to smell its saltiness.

Bees have been trained to use their extraordinary powers of smell to sniff out trouble for humans. Scientists at the Stealthy Insect Sensor Project at the Los Alamos National Laboratory have trained bees to be bomb detectors. When trained bees smell explosives, they stick out their long, curled tongues.

EXPERIMENT:

Smell Like a Bee

A bee's sense of smell is 100 times more powerful than a human's. Grab a friend and try this smelly experiment to see how your sniffer stacks up.

WHAT YOU NEED

- Plastic wrap
- Sharp pencil
- Bandana
- A friend to be your "bee"
- At least six to eight containers; you can use paper cups or reuse small, clean yogurt containers
- At least three or four strong-smelling items—like mints, oranges, lemons, cinnamon, garlic, pickles, honey, flowers, or vanilla extract

WHAT YOU DO

STEP 1:

Make your "flowers."

- Line up several pairs of containers. You're making two containers of each scent. Put something smelly in each container—don't mix!
- Cover each container tightly with plastic wrap and poke three holes in the top with a sharp pencil.

STEP 2:
Set up your smell garden.

○ Blindfold your "bee."

○ Place one of each scent on either side of a counter or table. Mix up the order of containers to make the game more challenging.

○ Have your bee smell the "flowers" on one side of the table or counter. Then guide them to the other side and have them smell those containers. Can they match the scents?

WHAT'S GOING ON?

This is how bees navigate the world of flowers and food gathering. They identify a specific scent of a flower and then go from one blossom to the next gathering nectar and pollen from that particular kind of flower.

What Does a Bee Feel?

Flowers have electric fields surrounding them. Not only can bees detect these electric fields, but they can also tell a lot about a flower before they even land on it by sensing the field's strength.

Bees are covered with tiny little hairs. As bees fly through the air, they fly into a lot of dust particles. The dust bumps into the little hairs on the bees' bodies and gives the bees small positive charges. A flower's electric field is negatively charged. When a positively charged bee flies near a negatively charged flower, things start jumping. Things like pollen.

At the base of each hair is a nerve that sends signals to the brain whenever the hair is moved. When a bee flies by a flower's electric field, it can tell whether the flower's negative charge is strong just by the way the field bends the hairs on its body. A weak field doesn't really move the hairs that much. This tells the bee to pass on by because another bee has already been there and feasted on pollen and nectar. A strong electric field from a flower really pulls on the hair and tells a bee there's plenty of food.

When a bee lands on a flower, the positive charge of the bee and the negative charge of the flower create a kind of magnet. The pollen, which also has a negative charge, leaps to the positively charged bee body and sticks.

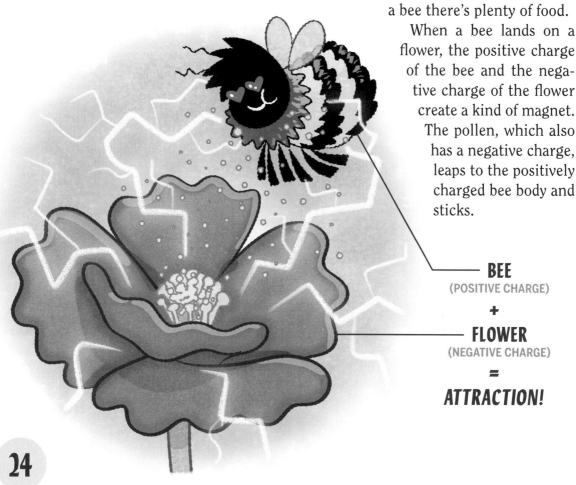

BEE
(POSITIVE CHARGE)

+

FLOWER
(NEGATIVE CHARGE)

=

ATTRACTION!

EXPERIMENT:

Leaping Pollen

Try this balloon-on-the-hair experiment to see how a charged bee body can make pollen leap from a flower.

WHAT YOU NEED

- Scissors
- Construction paper
- Tissue paper

- Balloon
- Your hair (or a fuzzy sweater)

WHAT YOU DO

STEP 1:

Make your flower.

- Use the scissors to cut a flower shape out of the construction paper.

STEP 2:

Make your pollen.

- Cut or tear the tissue paper into very small confetti-like pieces and make a pile in the center of your paper flower.

STEP 3:
Make the bee.

- Blow up your balloon and tie the end. This is your bee.

- Rub your bee on your sweater or on your hair for at least 10 seconds.

STEP 4:
Hunt for pollen.

- Hold your bee near the flower with the pollen but don't actually touch them together.

- What happens?

WHAT'S GOING ON?

When you rub the balloon "bee" on your hair or a fuzzy sweater, you are negatively charging it with an electric field.* The "pollen" confetti is slightly positively charged and the opposites attract. When you place the charged "bee" close to the "pollen," it leaps to the charged "bee."

* When you rub a balloon on your hair, it picks up electrons and makes the balloon negatively charged. In real life, a bee is positively charged because dust knocks electrons off of it.

Why Does a Bee Buzz?

A bee's wings move at an incredible 11,400 strokes per minute, and all that movement creates a real buzz. Bees buzz for a few other reasons as well. They buzz to communicate—to let creatures near them know they're around or to announce that they are alarmed or looking for a mate. Their buzz can also help them gather food. Some bees, like bumblebees, can amp up their buzz by shaking the muscles in their thorax and flapping their wings. When these bees land on a flower and buzz, the vibrations shake loose the pollen, which lands on the bee's body. Scientists call this "buzz pollination" or "sonication." Some flowers won't even give up their pollen until they are "buzzed" by a bee.

EXPERIMENT:

Movers and Shakers

You can use your own powers of buzzing to move stuff too.
Try this and see how humming can move mountains.

WHAT YOU NEED

- Plastic wrap
- A bowl
- Rubber band
- Marker
- ¼ teaspoon (1.2 mL) ground cinnamon

WHAT YOU DO

STEP 1:

Drape the plastic wrap over the opening of the bowl. Secure it with the rubber band to make a tight, drumlike surface. Gently draw a circle about the size of a penny in the middle with your marker.

STEP 2:

Place the cinnamon inside the circle.

STEP 3:

Put your face about a foot away from the surface. Make like a bee and hum.
What do you notice?

WHAT'S GOING ON?

The cinnamon in the center of the circle is like the pollen in a flower. When you hum at the surface of the plastic-wrapped bowl, or "flower," the vibrations of your voice make the surface shake. The shaking dislodges the cinnamon, or "pollen." This is similar to how a bee frees pollen from a flower when it buzzes nearby.

EXPERIMENT:

Buzz Off!

The buzz that a bee makes is a result of the quick movement of its wings. You can make your own bee buzzer and whip it around in the air to cause vibrations that sound just like a busy, buzzy bee.

WHAT YOU NEED

- Pencil erasers (the kind that fit over the end of a pencil)
- A wooden ice pop stick or craft stick
- A 3-inch-by-5-inch (76.2 by 127 mm) index card
- Stapler that's strong enough to staple the index card to the ice pop stick
- A 2-foot-long (0.6 m) piece of string
- A wide rubber band (about ¼ inch wide, or 6.4 mm) that's long enough to stretch lengthwise around the ice pop stick
- Scissors

WHAT YOU DO

STEP 1:

- Stick an eraser on each end of the ice pop stick.
- Then place the short edge of the index card along the length of the ice pop stick. (You may have to trim the card a bit to fit it between the erasers.)
- Staple the card in place with at least three staples.

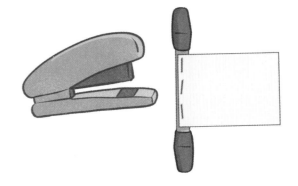

STEP 2:

- On one end of the stick, tie the string in a knot right under one eraser.
- Then stretch your fat rubber band from eraser to eraser. Make sure the string is coming out between the two sides of the rubber band.

STEP 3:

- Cut about ⅓ off the end of the index card.

STEP 4:

- Make the paper buzz by swinging the whole thing around in a circle by the string. Can you hear it?

WHAT'S GOING ON?

When you spin the bee buzzer, moving air causes the whole thing to vibrate. The index card and the rubber band flutter like a bee's wing and the vibrations make a sound just like the vibrating wings of a bee.

CHAPTER 3
PLANT POWER

Everything in our world comes back to plants. They create oxygen, which is important if you are used to breathing, and they're the basis of the food chain that feeds us and pretty much every other creature on the planet. Discover the mysteries of how plants do what they do and how bees help them keep going.

Making Food from Light—Go Green!

Plants are green for a reason. Their leaves are full of a pigment called *chlorophyll*. Chlorophyll soaks up the light from the sun, which plants use along with molecules from the air, soil, and water to make sugars that they use for food. This process is called *photosynthesis*. Only plants can do it. When we eat roots, fruits, stems, leaves and flowers, we're using the plant sugars for energy.

Chlorophyll looks green to us because that's the color of light that the plants don't use. Sunlight might look white, but it's made up of a bunch of different colors: red, orange, yellow, green, blue, indigo, and violet. The cells in plant leaves collect the red, orange, yellow, blue, and violet light energy from the sun and they reflect the green.

The Plants That Changed the World

Way back in the day, humans traveled in packs and hunted and gathered for food. It wasn't an easy life. Dinner could be anything from rats, woolly mammoth, or fish to berries, roots, or insects. People ate what they could find. And because they were on the go all the time, they were easy targets for saber-toothed tigers and other hungry animals that were also looking for food.

Then things changed. Humans started noticing the kinds of plants that were not only tasty but good for their health. They gathered more of them. They observed these plants and noticed patterns of growth, flowering, and rebirth. They connected the notion that the flowers and seeds, if planted, would grow into new plants. Boom! Agriculture was born. People started growing plants. They stopped needing to travel all the time. They built villages and traded crops. Civilization was born!

Today, civilization still counts on plants for survival and more. Aside from food and oxygen, wherever you are right now you can probably look around and see a plant-based thing. Wood and paper come from plants. Medicines come from plants. And you are probably wearing plants right now. Cotton, which makes up jeans and T-shirts, comes from plants.

EXPERIMENT:

Trace It Back

Everything you eat comes from a plant. Everything. Tracing a salad or a banana back to a plant is easy. They are plants, after all. Tracing a meat or dairy product to a plant is simple too. Animals eat plants. But what about some of the more complicated ingredients in the foods we eat, like cookies or even tacos? Try this experiment and see.

WHAT YOU NEED

- Your favorite food (a box of cereal, a peanut butter and jelly sandwich, a candy bar, sushi . . . you name it!)
- A piece of paper
- A pencil

WHAT YOU DO

STEP 1:

- Draw a line from the top of your paper to the bottom, right down the middle.
- On top of the left column, write "Ingredients." On the right column, write "Tracing It Back."

INGREDIENTS	TRACING IT BACK

STEP 2:

- Look at the label of your food item. If there is no label, then look at the food item carefully.

- Write down the list of ingredients in the left column.

STEP 3:

- Now look at each ingredient and see if you can trace it back to a plant. Write the plant name in the right column.

- Hint—anything with "ose" at the end is a sugar, and sugars come from plants like sugar cane, corn, and fruit.

INGREDIENTS	TRACING IT BACK
MARGARINE	SUNFLOWER
FLOUR	WHEAT
COCOA BUTTER	CACAO PLANT

WHAT'S GOING ON?

Every food you eat either comes from a plant, is made from a plant, or can be traced back through the food chain to a plant. But that doesn't mean that all foods are created equal. Foods that have been processed more, through factories and handling, are further away from the plants that they came from. For example, potato chips are not the same as fresh potatoes. For the most part, foods that have been processed the least are the most healthful.

Pollination Nation

No plant lives forever. Like most living things, plants need both male and female cells to come together to make more plants. It's a complicated process that starts with a flower.

Every flower has male and female parts. The male parts are called stamens and they produce pollen. The female part is called the pistil. Pistils are shaped like long vases. The rim is called the stigma and the base is called the ovary. Seeds are made at the bottom of the pistil in the ovules in the ovary. When pollen moves from the stamen to the pistil, fertilization occurs and a new plant seed is created. This process is called pollination.

But here's the rub: Pollination doesn't happen on its own. Plants can't move, so they need a little help. They rely on the wind or animals such as birds, bugs, and bees. These animals are called "pollinators." Lots of animals pollinate without even knowing it. They are drawn to flowers for their sweet nectar, and as they land on each flower they get covered with dusty pollen. The pollen sticks to the animal and goes along for the ride until it gets knocked off when the animal lands on another flower. Bringing pollen from one flower to another flower helps the flowers develop seeds and lets the plant pass along its genes to the next generation. The flowers offer something sweet to the pollinator in return. Everyone wins!

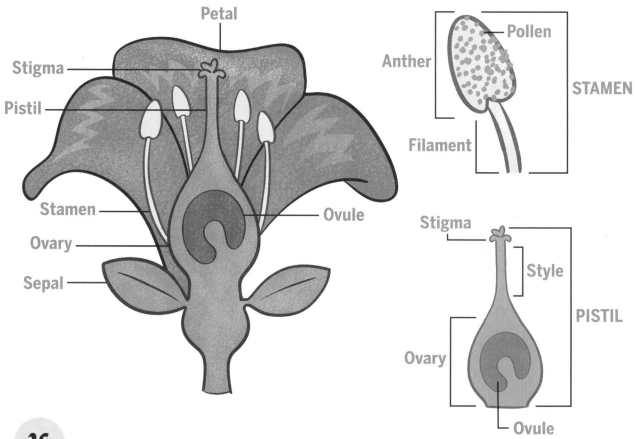

EXPERIMENT:
Dissect a Flower

Flowers are amazing! Pick a few and explore how they work. Use the diagram on page 36 for reference. Any type of flower will do, but it's nice to do this experiment with a couple of different flower varieties to compare. Daffodils, apple blossoms, and gladiolas work well.

WHAT YOU NEED

- Tape
- Pencil
- Scissors
- At least two sheets of thick paper—card stock is best, but poster board or cardboard work
- Flowers—at least two samples of any variety.

WHAT YOU DO

STEP 1:

Prepare your collection papers.

- Take a long piece of tape. Place it sticky side up across the middle of your paper from left to right.
- Use two small pieces of tape to secure it.
- This is your collection paper. Make one for each flower you are planning to examine.

STEP 2:

Take the flowers apart.

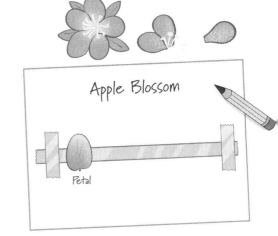

- At the top of your collection page, write the name of the flower.

- Pull off the petals. Look at them closely and place one on the tape on the far left side of the collection paper. Label this "petal."

- Find the sepal, pull it off, and place it on the collection paper next to the petal. Label this "sepal."

- Find the stamens, pull them off, and place one on the collection paper. Label this "stamen" and add "anther" and "filament."

- Find the pollen and stick some on your paper. Label this "pollen."

- Find the pistil, carefully cut it in half lengthwise, and place one half on the collection paper, cut side out. Add "pistil," "stigma," "style," "ovary," and "ovules" labels.

STEP 3:

Repeat steps 1 and 2 for the other kinds of flowers you have selected. How do the flowers compare? Are the parts easy to identify?

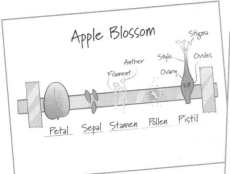

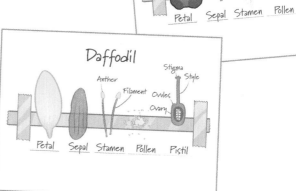

EXPERIMENT:
Cheetos Pollen

Use this orangey snack to see what happens during pollination.

WHAT YOU NEED

- Cheetos, the cheesier and more orangey, the better
- At least two paper cups
- At least two tissues (one for each cup)
- At least two rubber bands (one for each cup)
- Scissors

Don't have Cheetos? Use colored Jell-O dust or hot chocolate powder. Just dampen your fingers before you do **STEP 2**.

WHAT YOU DO

STEP 1:

Make your "flowers." You want to make at least two.

- Place a handful of Cheetos in each cup.

- Fold each tissue in half and make a 2-inch (5.1 cm) cut across the center. Open up each tissue and place one over the opening of each cup. Secure the tissue with a rubber band.

STEP 2:

Set your "flowers" up next to each other and be like a bee and pollinate.

- Trying not to tear the tissue, reach into one "flower" to grab the Cheetos, your "nectar." Enjoy your "nectar." But don't lick your fingers.
- Move to another cup, reach in, and collect more "nectar."
- Go back and forth a couple of times.
- What do you notice about your flowers?

WHAT'S GOING ON?

Just like a bee, you saw something in the "flower" that you wanted: a tasty treat. So you reached in and gathered it. And just like a flower, the Cheeto was covered with a dust. In the Cheeto's case, the dust is bright orange cheese. In the flower's case, the dust is pollen. When you go from cup to cup gathering your treat, the dust comes along for the ride on your fingers and gets rubbed off on the next cup. Your tissues became more and more orange. In nature, a bee gathers a treat and the pollen comes along for the ride. It gets rubbed off on the next flower and pollinates it—just like your orangey Cheeto dust.

Self-pollination vs. Cross-pollination

When pollen is transferred from a stamen to a pistil from the same plant, it is called *self-pollination*. When pollen is transferred from one plant to another, it is called *cross-pollination*. Cross-pollination produces stronger plants. The plants must be of the same species, however. For example, only pollen from a cherry tree can pollinate another cherry tree. Pollen from an apple tree could not pollinate a cherry tree.

The Who's Who of Pollinating

BEES: Pollen sticks to the hair on bees' bodies as they move from blossom to blossom gathering nectar and pollen. Honeybees are notoriously tidy, scraping pollen into carrying baskets on their legs and dropping only a few grains here and there. Mason bees, on the other hand, belly flop onto a flower. Pollen gets stuck all over their hairy bodies. Because they're covered in more pollen, they transfer more of it from flower to flower.

BUTTERFLIES: Butterflies prefer nectar from flat-faced flowers like sunflowers and daisies. As they land on each flower, some pollen rubs off onto their feet and they might carry it to the next flower.

BIRDS: Hummingbirds move so quickly and use so much energy that they have to eat nectar all day. They can visit up to 1,000 flowers a day, transferring pollen from each flower to the next.

BATS: Bats use their long tongues to suck up the nectar in flowers, and while they feast, pollen brushes up against their fur. Some of that pollen then gets knocked off on the next flower and pollinates it while the bat is enjoying its meal.

BEETLES AND OTHER INSECTS: Beetles and other insects may be drawn to the pollen and nectar of a flower. Like butterflies, they may transfer pollen from one bloom to the next and successfully pollinate plants.

WIND: Before any animals began eating flowers, plants depended on the wind to pollinate. They released pollen into the air and the wind would carry it to other flowers. Some plants like grass, grains, and evergreens still use this method.

No Bees, No Pizza

We know that bees help pollinate our favorite fruits and vegetables, but they also help things like alfalfa grass grow. While you may not be a chief consumer of alfalfa grass, the dairy cows that produce the cheese that goes on your pizza sure are. No bees mean no alfalfa, no cows, no cheese, no pizza. It's a domino effect. Not only will the cheese be affected, so will the tomatoes, green peppers, and olive oil. When you think about it, losing bees means losing ice cream too. No bees, no grass, no cows, no cream!

So, save the bees and keep the fabulous food!

A few things we wouldn't have if bees disappeared:

Alfalfa grass	Carrots	Eggplant	Peaches
Almonds	Cherries	Guava	Plums
Apples	Cocoa	Kiwi	Raspberries
Avocados	Coconuts	Lemons	Roses
Beans	Coffee	Limes	Strawberries
Blueberries	Cotton	Mangoes	Tomatoes
Broccoli	Cucumbers	Melons	Vanilla

CHAPTER 4

MEET THE MASON BEE

When it comes to pollination, bees are pros, and solitary bees, like the mason bee, are superstars.

There are about 150 different species of mason bees in the United States. One is the blue orchard mason bee. Just 250 blue orchard mason bees can pollinate an acre of fruit trees as effectively as 40,000 honeybees.

Warm-Up Colors

In general, mason bees are smaller than their bumblebee and honeybee cousins and are not always striped black and yellow. Blue orchard mason bees mostly appear to be all black, but when they catch the sunlight their fuzzy bodies give off a metallic blue or green sheen. Red mason bees are deep, dark red. Others are dark with tan fuzz. Mason bees are born, emerge from their nests, and start foraging on cool spring days. Their dark color helps them heat up in the sunshine. Even at a cool 55°F (12.7°C), the bees can begin to absorb the sun's rays and warm their muscles up enough to start moving.

Bee or Fly?

Bluebottle flies look a lot like blue orchard mason bees. They both have dark bodies that can look metallic in the sun. They both buzz. One giveaway is where they land. Mason bees are looking for nectar and pollen and are landing on flowers. Bluebottle flies are looking for garbage and are landing in the trash.

Gentle Bee

Mason bees almost never sting. Because they are solitary bees, they don't have a huge nest to protect and don't need heavy-duty defense strategies like venom and aggressive behavior. That's not to say they won't sting, however. If you pinch, squeeze, or really threaten a mason bee, she will defend herself. Luckily for you, a mason bee sting doesn't hurt like the sting of a bumblebee or a honeybee. Mason bees don't have venom, so their sting feels more like a mosquito bite.

Every Girl's a Queen

Unlike with social bees, every female mason bee is a queen. Like a single working mom, she does it all. She finds her own nest. She gathers her own food. She lays her eggs and protects them.

She even decides whether her eggs will develop into females or males. A female mason bee keeps the male's fertilizing cells in a separate pouch on her body. When laying her eggs, she decides when and if to use these cells. If she does use them, the egg will develop into a male. If she doesn't, the egg will become a female. Having this choice lets her place her female offspring deeper inside her nest. Why does location matter? A mason bee nest is shaped like a tube and divided into many different chambers, each with its own egg. Since male mason bees emerge from the nest several days before the females, it makes sense to have them closer to the exit.

Busy Baby Bees

In the spring, when sunlight begins to get stronger, growing mason bees begin to wiggle and wriggle inside their cocoons. The cocoons in the outer chambers of the nest, where the male bees are, feel the heat of the sun first. They wake up anywhere from 3 to 15 days before the females.

Once awake, a male mason bee munches his way out of his cocoon, staggers to the edge of his chamber, and hits a wall of dried mud. This is no problem for him. He just keeps chewing and doesn't stop until he chomps an opening in the wall and crawls out.

His wings are damp and cramped. He opens them in the fresh air and zips off to the nearest flower for his first meal. He feasts all day but never strays far from the nest. He is waiting for the females to emerge. Over the next few days, more males wake up and there is a men's club of bees sunning themselves and dining on nectar and pollen, waiting for the females.

A couple of days pass and finally females begin to come out of their chambers. They are larger than the males and their antennae are short and thick. They wiggle in the air. Their wings are damp and they cannot fly yet. The eager males immediately mate with them. Once their job is done, the males die.

Nesting Homebodies

After mating, a female immediately begins looking around the neighborhood for a new home to lay her eggs. Once a mason bee emerges from its cocoon, it never strays farther than a few hundred feet. Mason bees are solitary bees, but they like to live near each other. They build their nests in hollow, tube-shaped spaces like existing tunnels made by other insects in wood, the ground, hollow reeds, and even empty snail shells.

Belly-Flopping Foragers

Once she finds a safe place to lay her eggs, the mason bee creates the back wall for the nest cell. If she can't find the right materials for a back wall, like mud or damp soil, she won't be able to form a nest. But if all things are in place, she begins gathering food from flowers nearby.

When she lands, a mason bee pretty much body-slams the flower. Her full-body flop scatters a bunch of pollen, which is collected in hairy patches on her belly. She then mixes it with nectar to form a sticky lump. As she flies and flops from one blossom to the next, pollen showers off her body and sprinkles other flowers, pollinating them as she goes.

Wild Overachievers

Wild solitary bees like mason bees have been overlooked in the past by beekeepers because they don't produce honey. But the fact that they don't make honey makes mason bees amazing pollinators. Honeybees spend their time looking for nectar to convert into honey. They are picky about which flowers they visit. Mason bees, on the other hand, aren't picky at all.

No Time to Waste

The female takes the pollen-nectar lump back to her new nest and places it as far back as she can. She takes many trips gathering nectar and pollen to make a lump about the size of a large pea. Once she gets enough pollen and nectar gathered, she backs out of the nest, flips around, and backs all the way back in, down to the end. There she carefully lays a single tiny, sausage-shaped egg on top of the food lump.

Wall Building

After she lays an egg on the food lump, it's time for the bee to seal the egg chamber. She darts out of the nest, dips into some mud, and comes back. Using the mud, she seals off the egg chamber by creating a wall. This is what gives this type of bee its name: Mason bees, like masons, build walls.

From this point on, the egg is on its own. The mama bee has given it food and a safe space to grow. She flies off to gather more food to make more lumps and lay more eggs. Every egg has a room of its own.

In the end, her tube-shaped nest is a long line of sealed chambers. Each has a lump of food and a single egg. Each is sealed off with mud. The first eggs that a female lays at the back of the nest will be fertilized. They will develop into females. In the chambers closest to the front of the nest, the female lays unfertilized eggs. These will become males.

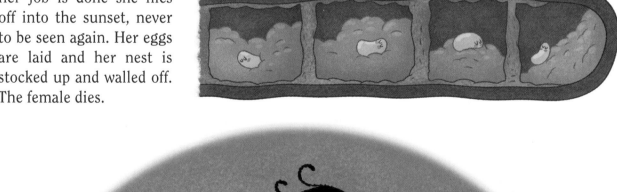

At a rate of about an egg a day, it takes a month for a mason bee to lay all of her eggs. When she's done, she builds a final thick mud wall to plug the nest and protect her babies as they grow. Once her job is done she flies off into the sunset, never to be seen again. Her eggs are laid and her nest is stocked up and walled off. The female dies.

Life Goes On

As the summer passes, there is much activity within the mason bee nest. The tiny, sausage-shaped egg flops onto the food lump. Then a larva emerges and begins to eat its way through the lump. Over the summer, the lump shrinks and the hungry larva grows.

Once the food is done, the larva starts to spin and weave a cocoon. Round and round it goes and overnight it turns from a chubby larva into a small brown cocoon. Inside the cocoon the larva changes into a pupa. The pupa stage is when most of the big changes occur. The pupa turns into an adult. (That's called *metamorphosis*.) Changes keep happening for weeks. By the end of the summer, a fully grown bee has developed inside the cocoon.

Fall passes. Winter passes. The new bees sleep inside their cocoons. One day the warming rays of the early spring sun begin to warm the nest. The bees start wiggling inside their cocoons and the whole cycle starts again.

STAGE 1: EGG

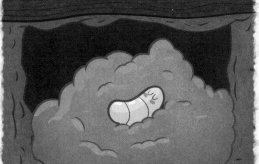

STAGE 2: LARVA

STAGE 3: COCOON

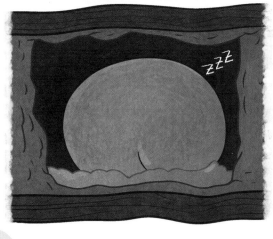

STAGE 4: ADULT

TURN THIS BOOK INTO A BEEHIVE!

CHAPTER 5

IF YOU BUILD IT, THEY WILL COME

Like people living in an apartment building, mason bees like to have their own private nesting place near where other mason bees live. In this chapter, you'll build your own beehive of paper nesting tubes. Each tube will be a single home for as many as 10 to 12 baby bees from a single female bee.

Turn This Book into a Beehive!

You can build a habitat for wild mason bees by creating a simple paper home out of this very book.

WHAT YOU NEED

- This book—specifically the jacket cover, the perforated pages that start on page 93, and the backing template on the last page of the book.
- Tape (Duct tape works best to keep the hive weatherproof.)
- Scissors

- A pencil, a thin marker, a chopstick, or any similar tool with a diameter of ³⁄₁₆ to ¼ inch (4.8 to 6.4 mm)
- String
- A sunny, covered place where you can hang the finished beehive
- A nail or hook for hanging

WHAT YOU DO

STEP I:

Make the beehive shell.

- Take the jacket cover off this book, turn it inside out, and match up the grommets with the holes.

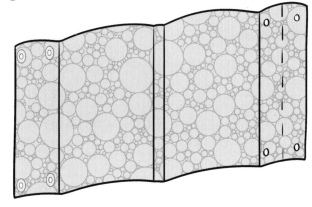

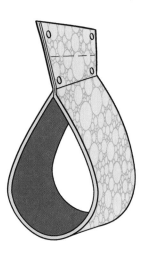

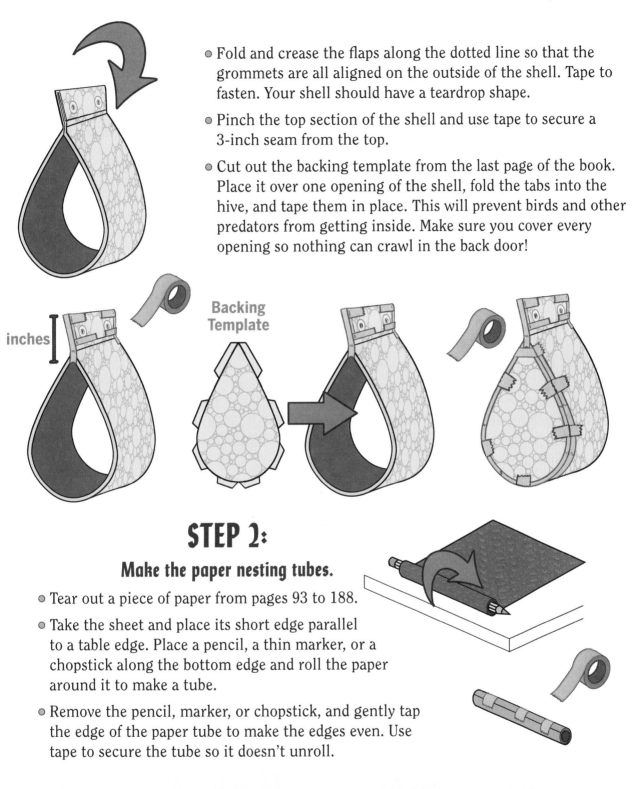

- Fold and crease the flaps along the dotted line so that the grommets are all aligned on the outside of the shell. Tape to fasten. Your shell should have a teardrop shape.
- Pinch the top section of the shell and use tape to secure a 3-inch seam from the top.
- Cut out the backing template from the last page of the book. Place it over one opening of the shell, fold the tabs into the hive, and tape them in place. This will prevent birds and other predators from getting inside. Make sure you cover every opening so nothing can crawl in the back door!

inches

Backing Template

STEP 2:

Make the paper nesting tubes.

- Tear out a piece of paper from pages 93 to 188.
- Take the sheet and place its short edge parallel to a table edge. Place a pencil, a thin marker, or a chopstick along the bottom edge and roll the paper around it to make a tube.
- Remove the pencil, marker, or chopstick, and gently tap the edge of the paper tube to make the edges even. Use tape to secure the tube so it doesn't unroll.

Different kinds of mason bees prefer tunnel-like spaces that range from ¼ inch to ⅝ inch (6.4 to 15.9 mm) wide and at least 6 inches (15.2 mm) deep. Leafcutter bees prefer slightly smaller tube diameters, around ³⁄₁₆ of an inch (4.8 mm) wide.

- Pinch the end of the tube and tape it shut. The tube can only have one entrance. If there's a back way in, parasitic wasps might creep in and take over the nest, using the pollen for their own babies.

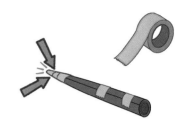

- Make a bunch of smaller tubes and a bunch of larger tubes. You'll need to make about 48 tubes total. If your tubes don't fit snugly in the shell, add more tubes.

- You may have to pinch the top seam of of the shell and tape it down more to make a snug fit.

Having some variation in size looks more natural and it gives the bees visual clues to figure out which tube is theirs.

STEP 3:

Put the beehive together.

- Place the paper nesting tubes inside the beehive shell, creating a random pattern of larger tubes and smaller tubes. Push the tubes all the way back, but stagger them slightly so that they stick out at different places.

- Tie a piece of string in a loop through the grommets in the shell.

- Hang your new hive in a sunny south- or east-facing sheltered area where it won't get wet if it rains. Place it at eye level so you can watch the comings and goings of your bees. And make sure there is a mud source nearby, as mason bees use mud to seal their egg chambers. Keep an eye on the mud source every day and make sure it doesn't dry out.

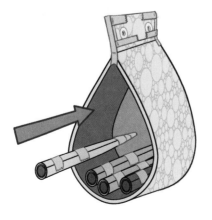
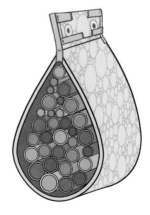

Location, Location, Location!

After you build a home for your bees, you need to put it in the right spot to attract them and entice them to stay. Mason bees need the warmth from the sun's rays to reach an interior muscle temperature of 80°F (26.7°C) so their wings will function, but if they get too hot, they'll bake to a crisp. Find a place facing south or east that gets morning sun. The morning sun will warm the bees so they can begin pollinating early in the day before it gets too hot. If you live in a warm-weather area, place your hive where it can get shade during the hottest part of the day.

Once you place your beehive, you can't easily move it, so make sure growing foliage won't eventually block the hive from sunshine. Don't place it near a bird feeder, either. A visiting bird may take it as an invitation to dine on your bees.

Finally, you want to keep your beehive out of the wind and rain, so make sure you hang it under an overhang or create a roof of your own.

Bee Food

You'll need to make sure there's enough food to keep your mason bees around when they emerge in the spring. There should be blossoming plants within a couple of hundred feet of your hive. And since bees are around from March through October, you want to design a garden that will keep them happy, interested, and fed all spring, summer, and fall. Pick plants that blossom at different times of the year. That way, as one flower dies off another flower can provide nectar and pollen for your bees. Make big patches of flowers and don't worry about pruning and being too fussy. Bees like it wild.

The best plants for your bees are the ones that grow naturally in your area. Fruit trees (cherries, apples, and oranges) are always a good bet, as are blueberry bushes. Go to local garden centers or nurseries and take a look at what kinds of flowers are out in early spring. And don't be afraid to ask what flowers they think bees seem to like the best.

Finally, color counts when you are planting for bees. Since bees can't see red, red flowers aren't very interesting to them unless they have ultraviolet patterns as well (unfortunately, we can't see ultraviolet). In general, most bees love purple, blue, white, and yellow flowers.

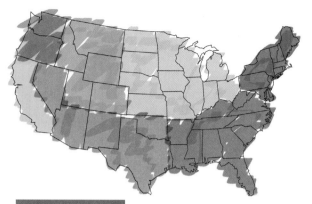

Mason Bee Blooms

Here is a region-by-region snapshot of some native plants that bloom in the spring and might delight your bees.

SOUTHEAST

Redbud

Honeysuckle

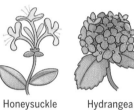
Hydrangea

Sunflower

Pawpaw

MIDWEST

Phlox

Willow

Prairie Clover

Sumac

Black-Eyed Susan

ROCKIES

Columbine

American Vetch

Bee Balm

Indian Paintbrush

Prairie Bluebell

NORTHEAST

Dogwood

Kinnikinnick

Violet

Witch Hazel

PACIFIC NORTHWEST

Hazelnut Tree

Trillium

Blackberry

Vine Maple

WEST COAST

Poppy

Lupine

Thistle Sage

Milkweed

SOUTHWEST

Terrybear Cholla

Mesquite

Cactus Apple

And here is a short list of bee-happy plants based on blooming season. Find out which grow best in your area and plant at least one that blossoms in each season. You'll attract a number of different species of bees, butterflies, and other pollinators.

SPRING: barberry, bee plant, blanket flower, blazing star, blue pea, borage, bush anemone, calendula, California poppy, Chinese houses, crocus, daisy, horehound, hyacinth, lavender, lilac, marigold, sage, salvia, scented geranium, tansy, wisteria, yarrow

SUMMER: basil, bee balm, bidens, black-eyed Susan, bluebeard, catnip, chaparral nightshade, cosmos, dusty miller, echinacea, goldenrod, gum plant, hosta, lamb's ear, lemon queen, mint, oregano, pincushion, purple coneflower, rosemary, sage, sea holly, sedum, snapdragon, spearmint, sunflower, thyme, toadflax, tomato, verbena, witch hazel, yarrow, zinnia, zucchini

AUTUMN: autumn sage, pumpkin, squash, yellow trumpet bush

Reduce Poisons

Some chemicals that eliminate pests and weeds are actually poisons. They kill off what we're trying to get rid of, but they're not great for people, pets, or your garden. And they can be downright deadly to bees, butterflies, birds, and other helpful critters.

There are a bunch of natural products that keep your garden weed- and pest-free without endangering everything else. Many can be found in your kitchen cupboard. Sprinkling white vinegar on weeds will knock them out. Spraying a mix of biodegradable dish soap and water on plants can get rid of slugs and aphids. And you can introduce ladybugs, spiders, and praying mantises into your garden to get rid of creatures that munch on your veggies.

ACTIVITY:

Spray It!

Here are a handful of easy-on-the-planet solutions for keeping your garden pest-free. You can whip up these recipes with materials you probably already have lying around the house. For each one you will need a sprayer.

Garlic Spray

Gets rid of aphids, spider mites, and whiteflies

WHAT YOU NEED

- 1 whole garlic bulb
- 2 cups (500 mL) water
- Blender
- Empty 2-liter bottle with cap
- Cheesecloth
- Rubber band
- Fresh water

WHAT YOU DO

STEP 1:

Put the garlic and the 2 cups (500 mL) of water in the blender. Whip at high speed until the garlic is pureed. Pour the mixture into the 2-liter bottle, put the cap on, and let it sit overnight.

STEP 2:

Open the bottle, place cheesecloth over the mouth, and secure it with a rubber band. Pour out the contents into the sprayer, leaving the garlic pulp behind. Fill the sprayer halfway. Use fresh water to fill the rest of the sprayer and tighten the lid.

STEP 3:

Spritz the tops and bottoms of leaves and the stems thoroughly.

STEP 4:

Reapply once a week and after a rain.

Spicy Spray

*Gets rid of furry
four-legged creatures*

WHAT YOU NEED

- 2 teaspoons (10 mL) cayenne pepper
- 1 tablespoon (15 mL) chili powder
- 2 teaspoons (10 mL) dry mustard
- 1 tablespoon (15 mL) Tabasco sauce
- 1 quart (0.9 L) warm water

WHAT YOU DO

STEP 1:

Mix the ingredients and pour
into the sprayer.

STEP 2:

Spritz all around the border
of your garden.

STEP 3:

Reapply after watering or a
rain as needed.

Baking Soda Spray

*Gets rid of powdery mildew
and other fungi*

WHAT YOU NEED

- 3 tablespoons (45 mL) baking soda
- 1 tablespoon (15 mL) biodegradable liquid dish soap
- 1 quart (0.9 L) water

WHAT YOU DO

STEP 1:

Mix the ingredients and pour
into the sprayer.

STEP 2:

Remove leaves that are
seriously infested.

STEP 3:

Spritz all parts of the plant
that seem affected.

STEP 4:

Reapply every other week.

Garlic, Onion, and Pepper Spray

Gets rid of cabbage worms, caterpillars, hornworms, aphids, flea beetles, and other insects

WHAT YOU NEED

- 6 cloves garlic
- 1 onion, minced
- 1 tablespoon (15 mL) hot pepper flakes
- 1 quart (0.9 L) hot water
- Blender
- Empty 2-liter bottle with cap
- 1 teaspoon (5 mL) biodegradable liquid dish soap
- Cheesecloth
- Rubber band

WHAT YOU DO

STEP 1:

Put the garlic, onion, pepper, and water in the blender. Whip at high speed until everything is pureed. Pour the mixture into the 2-liter bottle. Add the dish soap, put the cap on, and let it sit overnight.

STEP 2:

Open the bottle, place cheesecloth over the mouth, and secure it with a rubber band. Pour out the contents into the sprayer, leaving the pulp behind.

STEP 3:

In the morning when the plants are damp, spritz tops and bottoms of leaves as well as stems.

Milk Spray

Gets rid of powdery mildew and other fungi

WHAT YOU NEED

- 2 cups (500 mL) milk
- 2 cups (500 mL) water

Soap Spray

Gets rid of aphids, spider mites, and whiteflies

WHAT YOU NEED

- 1 tablespoon (15 mL) biodegradable liquid dish soap
- 1 quart (0.9 L) water

WHAT YOU DO

STEP 1:

Mix the ingredients and pour into the sprayer.

STEP 2:

Spritz all parts of the plant that seem affected.

STEP 3:

Reapply every week for three weeks.

WHAT YOU DO

STEP 1:

Mix ingredients and pour into sprayer.

STEP 2:

Spritz the tops and bottoms of leaves as well as the stems.

STEP 3:

Reapply after watering or a rain as needed.

Down and Dirty

Mason bees need mud to create the walled chambers that contain their eggs. It has to be the right kind of mud too. If the mud is too dry or too chunky they can't carry it. Mud with gravel, bark, or sand is a no-go.

If you have a yard, find a place where you can dig a small hole near the beehive. Make sure the hole is deep enough so you can see the different layers of soil. Mason bees prefer the claylike soils found just under the surface.

If you don't have a yard or if your beehive is in the city on a fire escape or roof, no worries! You can make your own mudhole. Just get a shovelful of mud that has particles smaller than sand. Keep the mud in a nearby bucket and keep it moist. The bees will do the rest.

A Little Sip

Bees need water just like any animal. But too much water can be deadly. Don't leave buckets of open water out around your hive. Bees can swoop in for a sip and drown by accident. Instead, take a shallow dish and fill it with only about an inch (a couple centimeters) of water. Add a few waterproof items: marbles, sticks, stones, shells, or sea glass. Whatever you use, make sure it sticks out of the water. This gives the bees a few things they can land on, use to get close to the water, and climb out on if they fall in.

ACTIVITY:

Build a Bee Bath

Bees need a place to get fresh, clean water.
Here's a simple bee bath you can build.

WHAT YOU NEED

- A shallow dish with a rim
- Pebbles, sticks, twigs, marbles, and/or plastic items that bees can land on
- Water

WHAT YOU DO

STEP 1:

Find a nice shady spot near your hive to place the bee bath.

STEP 2:

Fill a dish with pebbles or twigs or marbles . . . anything that won't dissolve in water and can be a nice landing pad for bees.

STEP 3:

Pour water into the dish. Make sure not to fill it so deep that the bees don't have a place to perch above the waterline while drinking.

STEP 4:

Check it every day and refill when necessary.
Bees need water every day.

Protect Your Hive from Pests

Plenty of creatures see a mason bee nest as a tasty treat full of yummy cocoons. To keep your bees safe, you may have to protect them from a variety of hungry beasts. Here are two of the most common:

SQUIRRELS: If squirrels are raiding the hive, you can place the whole thing in a sturdy box with a hole in the front. The hole should be big enough so that bees can come and go, but small enough that squirrels will be kept out.

BIRDS: You can protect the hive with chicken wire to prevent birds from digging into the tubes. Place the chicken wire at least 2 inches (5.1 cm) from the tube entrances—birds like woodpeckers have long tongues. And don't put your bee house near the bird feeder!

Mason Bee Hives Through the Seasons

There is a lot to think about year-round for your mason bees. Here's a season-by-season guide to keeping your hive thriving.

SPRING: The days are getting longer, leaves are peeping out, and flower buds are starting to appear. When the temperature hits the low 70s (low 20s Celsius) for a few days in a row, spring is springing! Keep an eye on the blossoms of trees in your area. If they are budding, it's time to act. Your hive needs to be in place and prepared for your bees before anything blooms. Depending on where you live, this can be as early as February or as late as May. Mason bees emerge at the beginning of spring and are busy for a good 5 to 6 weeks.

SUMMER: Long, warm days and short, cool nights mean summertime. The mason bees have done their work. They have gathered pollen and nectar, pollinated plants, and laid eggs in their nests. Now the cocoons are busy growing inside the hive. Protect those developing mason bee larvae. Make sure the hive is safe from squirrels, birds, and predatory insects and isn't getting overheated. If temperatures really start to bake, you may need to keep the hive shaded during the hottest part of the day.

Although adult mason bees are done with their work in the summer, leafcutter bees are just getting started. Leafcutter bees, like mason bees, are solitary and also lay their eggs in tubes. But instead of using mud to seal off their egg chambers, they make walls with chewed-up leaves. Keep an eye on your hive to see if you have any leafcutter bees making their home there. They're welcome to stay!

FALL AND WINTER: The days are getting shorter and the temperature starts falling. Within your hive, the cocoons have changed. Inside each one is a mature bee waiting to emerge in the spring. The cold will not harm them. They will sleep through the winter months. Just make sure the hive is protected from severe weather and let nature take its course.

Some mason beekeepers actually harvest their hives in the fall. They collect the tubes, slit them open, and gather the cocoons. They then carefully wash the cocoons to remove fungus, mites, and other pests and store them in a cool, dark, protected place for the winter, like in a paper bag in the refrigerator. It's not necessary to do this. Just make sure you set out a clean, new hive in the spring for the next generation of mason bees. If you have removed your cocoons and kept them in the refrigerator, take them out when the temperature reaches into the 50s (low teens Celsius). Place them near a clean hive and tear a small hole in the bag. The bees will emerge when they are ready.

REMEMBER: Bees are wild insects! They may not always cooperate. They may not nest in your hive the first year. They may get gobbled up by a bird. They may never emerge from their cocoons. Nature is unpredictable. Keep trying! If you don't have any luck attracting wild locals, you can also purchase mason bees from a garden store or local beekeeper.

Construction Zone

So you've already turned your book into a beehive and you want to make more bee houses? You're in luck! As long as there are clean, hollow spaces, mason bees can make their nests out of almost anything. Turn the page for a bunch of different hives you can create. You'll need to put a fresh one out every spring.

ACTIVITY:

Wood Condo

This hive is a great way to use old pieces of wood you may have around the house. Just don't use pressure-treated wood, as the chemicals could harm the bees. You can paint your hive any color or leave it au naturel.

WHAT YOU NEED

- Grown-up to help
- Thick block of untreated wood, at least 7 inches deep (17.8 cm)
- A flat piece of wood (for the roof) that is about ¼ inch (.6 cm) thick and measures larger than the footprint of the thick block. (If your thick block of wood measures 4 inches by 4 inches by 7 inches, the flat piece should be at least 5 inches by 8 inches, or 12.7 cm by 20.3 cm.)
- Clamp
- Drill with different size drill bits measuring up to 10 mm diameter
- Sandpaper
- Hammer
- Four flat-head two-penny nails (about 1 inch/2.5 cm long)
- 1 to 2 feet (0.6 to 0.9 m) sturdy wire or string
- Acrylic or other non toxic paint and brushes (optional)

WHAT YOU DO

STEP 1:

- Secure your thick wood block to a workbench with a clamp.
- Ask an adult to help drill several holes into the wood, at least 6 inches deep.
- Try different size holes, ranging from 3 mm to 6 mm wide, to offer a variety to the bees. Make sure the holes are at least 1 inch (2.5 cm) apart and go the length of the deepest part of the wood, but not out the other side.
- Use the sandpaper to smooth the wood at the entrance of each hole.

64   TURN THIS BOOK INTO A BEEHIVE!

STEP 2:

- Position the flat piece of wood on top of the wood block so it creates an overhanging roof in the front to protect the holes from the weather.
- It shouldn't overhang the block at the back so the block can sit flat against a wall.

STEP 3:

- Use the hammer and nails to secure the flat piece of wood to the block.
- Make sure you leave the heads of the nails sticking out a little.

STEP 4:

- Attach the string or wire to the two back nails. You will use this for hanging your beehive.

STEP 5:

- Paint your bee house if you like.

STEP 6:

- Hang or place your hive at eye level in an east- or south-facing spot in open sun.

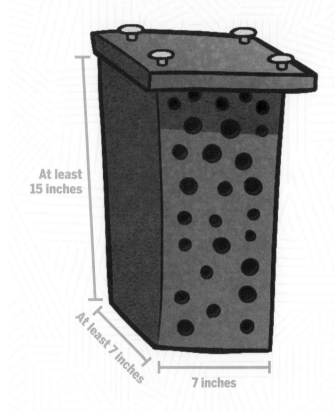

At least
15 inches

At least 7 inches

7 inches

Totally Tubular Bamboo Bungalow

Bamboo is perfect for mason bees to make their homes in. The walls are tough and waterproof, and they come in a variety of sizes. If you don't have any growing in your yard, you can easily find bamboo at gardening centers. Buy it in longer lengths and cut them into the size you need.

WHAT YOU NEED

- Grown-up to help
- A bunch of bamboo canes at least 8 inches (20.3 cm) long—the diameter should be about ¼ inch (6.4 mm) wide.
- Ruler
- Felt-tip pen
- A saw
- Drill
- 3 to 4 feet (0.9 to 1.2 m) pliable wire for wrapping the canes together
- Paper
- Duct tape

WHAT YOU DO

STEP 1:

- Measure and mark the bamboo canes into at least a dozen 8-inch-long (20.3 cm) pieces.
- Ask an adult to help saw the canes into tubes. Make sure all the bamboo tubes are hollow. If there are any blockages, ask an adult to help clear them with the drill.

STEP 2:

- Gather the bamboo together and tap the ends so they are even.
- Twist wire around the front, the middle, and the end of the bundle to secure the tubes.

STEP 3:

- For each tube, scrunch up a wad of paper and tuck it in the back to create a wall.
- Then place duct tape over the end so it is completely sealed.

STEP 4:

- Hang or place your hive at eye level in a protected east- or south-facing spot in open sun.

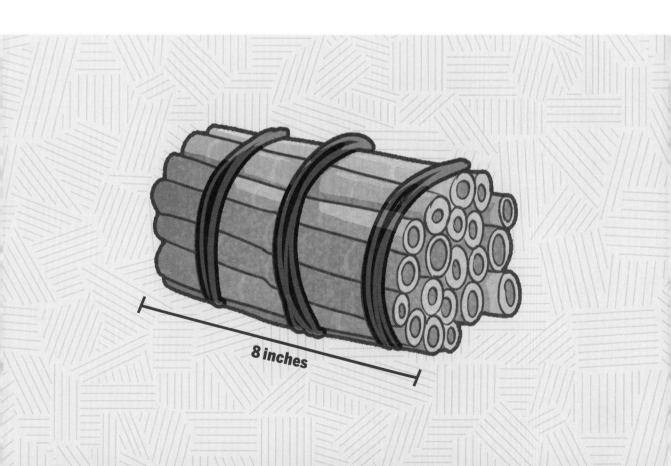

8 inches

ACTIVITY:

Stem House

Many species of solitary bees prefer a more natural variety of tube sizes. Experiment with dried hollow stems of different plants. Reeds, hollow grasses, and raspberry canes can be cut up and bundled to make beehives with different size openings.

WHAT YOU NEED

- Dried hollow stems at least 8 inches (20.3 cm) long
- Ruler
- Marker
- Scissors
- Sandpaper
- String
- Cardboard
- Pencil
- Duct tape

WHAT YOU DO

STEP 1:

- Measure and mark the hollow stems into at least 20 8-inch-long (20.3-cm-long) pieces.
- With your scissors, snip the stems into tubes. Make sure the cuts are clean and without splinters that can harm bees.
- If the edges feel rough, you can use sandpaper to smooth them.

STEP 2:

- Gather the stems into a bundle about the diameter of a coffee mug.
- Tie the bundle near the front, in the middle, and near the end with string.

STEP 3:

- ◎ Place the bundle on one end of the cardboard and trace around it.
- ◎ Cut out the cardboard shape and tape it to the end of the bundle to create a back wall.

STEP 4:

- ◎ Place your bundle in a woodpile, under bricks or stones, or even in a clay pot set on its side for shelter. The stems must be kept completely dry or they will rot, so make sure to push them in far enough so the openings are protected from the elements.
- ◎ Replace the stems every year or two.

ACTIVITY:

Pop Bottle Beehive

You can make an inviting beehive with recyclables! Find a plastic pop bottle and some paper straws (or plain paper) and make a perfectly pleasant mason bee home.

WHAT YOU NEED

- Grown-up to help
- Plastic pop bottle (1- or 2-liter)
- Scissors
- Paper straws (or paper you can roll around a pencil into straws). You'll need anywhere from 20 to 40, depending on the size of the bottle you are using. Aim for each tube to be at least 8 inches long. (You can also use hollow grasses, reeds, or bamboo, if you like.)
- A skein of wool yarn—or an old wool sweater can work in a pinch
- Pencil
- An egg-size ball of air-dry clay like Play-Doh (or mud)
- Tape
- String or wire

WHAT YOU DO

STEP 1:

- Ask a grown-up to help you cut the top off the pop bottle at the shoulder, where the bottle starts to narrow.

STEP 2:

- Gather the straws into a bundle and wrap it with yarn.
- Make sure you have a good ¼ to ½ inch (6.4 to 12.7 mm) wide wrapping of yarn around the bundle. If you don't have yarn, you can cut up an old sweater and wrap that around the bundle.

STEP 3:

○ Place a ball of clay or mud inside the pop bottle, as deep as you can.

STEP 4:

○ Push the bundle firmly into the clay.

STEP 5:

○ Place your hive at eye level in a protected east- or south-facing spot in open sun.

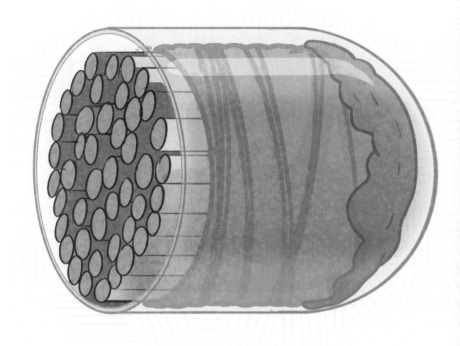

Take It Further

Make two pop bottle beehives and paint them. Paint one a light color and the other a darker color. Place them in similar spots, not too near each other, and see if one is more attractive to the mason bees.

CHAPTER 6

SAY HI TO THE HONEYBEE

In contrast to solitary bees, honeybees are highly social. They live in colonies that consist of one queen and all her children. They divide up labor, store food, and work together to keep the colony thriving. A honeybee colony can even be thought of as a single being—a superorganism—where all the parts work together for the benefit of the whole.

Family Structure

A honeybee colony includes three types of bees: worker bees, drones, and the queen. With each bee performing a specific job, the colony is a well-organized village.

Worker bees are all females. They are, as their name suggests, the workers of the colony. They do everything from building, cleaning, and protecting the nest to foraging for nectar and pollen, creating honeycomb, making honey, packing pollen, taking care of the eggs, and keeping the queen fed and cool.

Drones are the males. They have one job—to mate with the queen. Once they do, they drop to the ground and die.

The queen is the largest bee in the colony and the layer of all the eggs. She lays about 2,000 a day. Most bees have a life span of less than a year, but the honeybee queen can live for up to five years. However, this doesn't mean she's in charge. If the queen doesn't lay enough eggs, the colony can get rid of her and put a new queen in place.

WORKER

DRONE

QUEEN

Hive Sweet Hive

Every honeybee nest and hive is made up of rows of six-sided, or hexagon-shaped, cells. A bunch of these cells together is called honeycomb.

Honeycomb is made of beeswax. To make beeswax, worker bees gorge on honey. As they keep eating, a waxy substance comes out of their bodies and hardens into small flakes. The bees chew up the flakes and turn them into a soft material that they shape into cells around their bodies.

If you look at a honeycomb you'll see that each six-sided cell is exactly the same size—big enough to hold the body of a single bee. This is no accident. It takes 6 to 7 pounds (2.7 to 3.2 kg) of honey to make 1 pound (0.5 kg) of beeswax. So bees want to use it wisely. They've engineered the most efficient shape to hold the largest amount of stuff with the least amount of beeswax. If the cells were circular, there would be lots of wasted space in between them. Triangular cells fit together but use more beeswax. Hexagonal cells, however, fit together perfectly with no wasted space in between them and use the least amount of wax to make.

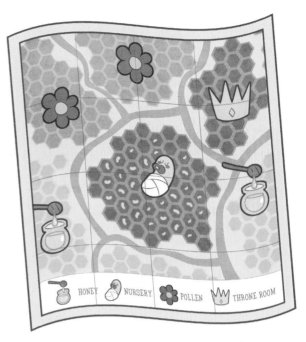

HONEY   NURSERY   POLLEN   THRONE ROOM

Honeycomb cells contain different things depending on where in the nest they're located. In the center of the nest are the nursery cells. This is where the eggs are laid and where they develop into adult bees. Surrounding these cells are chambers filled with honey. Around the outer edge are cells filled with pollen. The overall shape of the pattern in beehives is called the brood pattern. Beekeepers study this pattern and get information about the health of their colony.

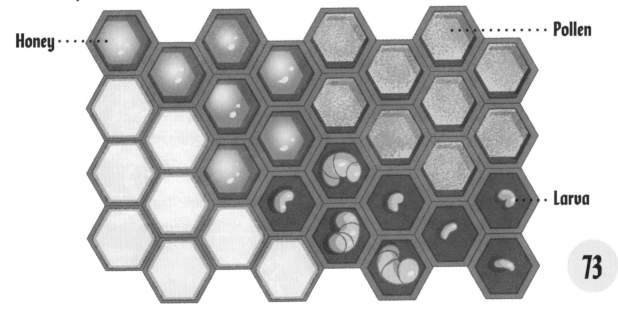

Honey · · · · · · · ·   · · · · · · · · · · · Pollen

· · · · Larva

73

Honeycomb Hexagons

Bees are some of nature's most amazing engineers. They build their homes out of shapes that create the greatest amount of storage from the least amount of material. Make your own honeycomb and see why hexagons are a magical shape.

WHAT YOU NEED

- Two paper towel cardboard tubes
- Ruler
- Pencil
- Scissors
- Glue
- Paper clips
- Spray paint (optional)

WHAT YOU DO

STEP 1:

Make your cells.

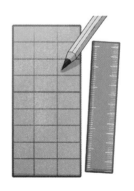

- Squash and smooth your cardboard tubes so they lie flat. Place a ruler at the top of each tube and use your pencil to divide the width into three equal segments, each about ¾ inch (1.9 cm). Turn the tube upside down and make the same marks on the other end.

- Use your pencil and ruler to draw two straight lines down the length of the tube connecting the marks on the top and bottom. Now measure along the length of the tube, marking off ¾-inch (1.9 cm) segments as you go. You should end up with a graph paper–like look.

- Use the scissors to cut across the width at these lines. You will end up with a bunch of ¾-inch (1.9 cm) strips, which slightly open to a football shape.

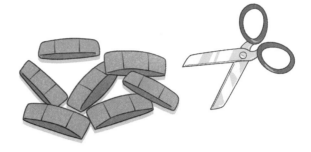

STEP 2:
Put your cells together.

- Take a few strips and open them up to form them into circles. Place the circles next to each other as if you were making honeycomb. What do you notice?

- Now flatten your circles again and fold each at the lines to make Z-shaped folds. Make sure to really crease the folds.

- Open up your strips and form them into hexagons. (You'll have to reverse some of the folds.) Place the hexagons next to each other as if you were making honeycomb. What do you notice? How does it compare with how the circles fit together?

- Glue your honeycomb together. Secure the glued sides with paper clips overnight or until they dry. If you want to, paint your honeycomb and hang it on the wall after it dries.

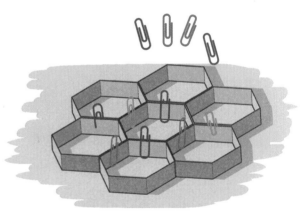

WHAT'S GOING ON?

When you place the circles together, you can see all the wasted space between them. But the hexagons fit together perfectly with no wasted space. The shape holds the most and needs the least amount of material to create it.

Power of the Colony

All of the bees in a colony depend on each other. They each have jobs to do. Here is a list of some worker bee roles. They fall under two categories: forager bees and nest bees.

FORAGER BEES make their way out of the nest to either protect it or search for food.

NEST BEES stick around the nest. They make wax, build honeycomb, gather nectar from foragers to create honey, and keep the nest clean and temperate.

COURT BEE
This bee stays within antenna distance from the queen at any given moment. She makes sure the queen is fed, clean, warm, dry, healthy, and producing eggs.

FANNING BEE
This bee uses her wings to cool the queen, keep the eggs cold in hot months, fan the honey so it evaporates and becomes the right consistency, or keep the nest at the perfect temperature and dryness.

GUARD BEE
This bee is the colony's first line of defense. She stands watch, attacks intruders, and warns the colony if there's danger.

FORAGER BEE
This bee gets the information from the forager scout and takes off to find the flowers. She returns with a belly full of nectar or baskets full of pollen to give to a worker bee. A forager specializes in either water, nectar, or pollen.

NURSE BEE
This bee takes care of the eggs and developing larvae.

FORAGER SCOUT
This bee explores the neighborhood looking for flowers and other food sources. She then flies back to the colony to report back.

UNDERTAKER BEE
This bee keeps the place clean. She gathers the bodies of dead bees that could spread infection and carries them to the opening of the nest, where she tosses them out.

Growing Up a Worker Bee

A worker bee doesn't have the same job her whole life. She moves through the ranks as she ages. From birth to 21 days, all worker bees work inside the nest. First, they work in the nursery keeping the place clean and warm. After a few days, they begin feeding the older larvae, then the youngest. After about two weeks, they move on to new tasks elsewhere in the nest.

At three weeks, workers begin to venture outside. They take up guard and after around 20 to 40 days begin foraging for food. Worker bees have a life span of about six weeks. Since there are always younger bees coming up through the ranks, the different jobs are always taken care of.

Honeybee Life Cycle

Every bee starts as an egg. But not all eggs are the same. Eggs that have been fertilized become female. Most of them become worker bees. A few might become queens if the conditions are right. Eggs that are not fertilized become males, or drones. Every egg is laid in its own honeycomb chamber.

It takes about three days for an egg to hatch into a larva. All larvae are fed the same food. Nurse bees in charge of feeding have special glands in their heads that turn pollen into a rich food called royal jelly. They spit it all over the larvae. After a couple of days, the larvae grow and their food is switched to a mixture of pollen and honey, unless the larva is meant to be a queen.

When a queen hatches into a larva, she is also bathed in royal jelly. She will be fed it her whole life. Her food will not be diluted with honey and pollen. As a result she will grow bigger and faster than the other larvae.

As a larva grows, it gets too big for its outer skin and needs to molt. The old skin splits and sheds to let the larva develop. After the fourth molting, a nurse bee caps the cell with beeswax.

Inside the cell, the larva spins a cocoon around itself. It's no longer a larva. Now it is a pupa. Inside the cocoon, the pupa develops into an adult bee. The whole process takes about ten days for a worker bee and six days for a queen. When it's ready, the adult bee chews its way out of its cell. Its wings unfold and harden in the air. It's off to start work.

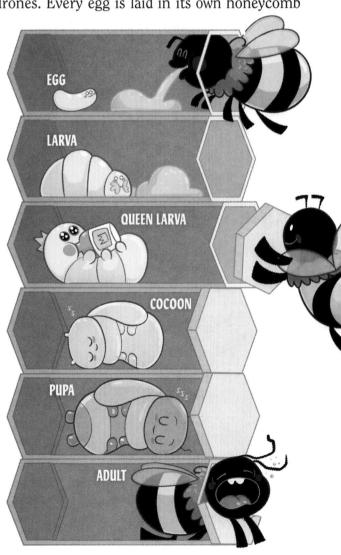

EGG

LARVA

QUEEN LARVA

COCOON

PUPA

ADULT

A Year in the Life of a Honeybee Colony

Honeybee colonies are active places all year round. Here's a season-by-season look at the action.

Fall and Winter

When fall and winter arrive, some animals hibernate and some fly south. Bees stick around and stay close together in the nest.

Throughout the cold months, less food comes into the nest and most of the older bees die off. The remaining young, healthy workers cluster around the queen, keeping her warm and fed with stored honey. They pack around her so tightly that they actually form a ball. This ball is called a winter cluster, and it keeps her a cozy 85° to 90°F (29.4° to 32.2°C).

The worker bees create heat by vibrating their wings. But their wings aren't moving at all. They unhook their body muscles from their wings so the vibrations produce only muscle movement and heat and no wing movement.

In order to keep the heat up, the worker bees need plenty of honey for energy. The bees on the outside of the cluster reach cells packed with honey and refuel. Eventually those bees move their way to the inside and other bees move to the outer edges to feed. This way the bees all feed and stay warm.

Spring

When the temperatures warm up, the queen begins to lay her eggs. The eggs she lays in the beginning are all female. Female bees are the workers in the colony and the most essential to its survival. Later, when the population of the colony is greater, the queen will begin laying male eggs.

The colony will expand quickly. At its height, a honeybee nest can house around 50,000 bees. As the nest starts to get overcrowded, workers begin preparing new queens. Normal eggs that would simply develop into workers are separated and fed royal jelly. Since every colony can have only one queen, this activity means that the colony must be split in two.

Just before the new queens are about to emerge from their cells, the old queen takes off. About two thirds of all the bees in the colony go with her. This is called a swarm. The swarm gathers on a nearby tree branch and waits for scouting bees to return with information on a new nest site. The swarm then flies to the new spot, builds a nest, finds food, and makes honeycomb and honey, and the queen immediately starts laying eggs.

Back at the old colony, workers get ready for the new queen to begin her reign. When a new queen emerges from her cocoon, she searches the nest for any other emerging queens. Mortal combat ensues and one queen survives. She flies out of the nest and mates with drones. The drones die and she returns to the nest. Worker bees feed, groom, and take care of her. In two to three days, she begins laying eggs.

Summer

The days are long and hot and the bees spend them gathering nectar and pollen and creating honey to store for the winter. But no matter what temperature it is outside, the inside of the nest stays around a toasty 95°F (35°C).

At the first sign of overheating, the nest bees communicate with special water forager bees. They stick their tongues in the water forager bees' mouths to tell them that water is needed. The forager bees then fly off in search of water to cool the nest. When a water forager comes back, its crop (also called a honey stomach) is filled with water. It transfers the water to a nest bee, who spreads the cooling water over the warm surfaces inside the nest. Other bees move to the edge of the nest and begin fanning their wings. This evaporates the water, moves the hot air out of the nest, and gets rid of extra humidity, keeping the nest cool and dry.

As fall approaches, the bees prepare the colony for winter. They need to have adequate honey stores to survive the coming months. Older bees begin to die off, and younger bees gather around the queen to keep her warm and fed through the winter. The cycle continues.

Beat the Heat

Flapping wings can help water evaporate more quickly and cool things down. Try this experiment and see if you can beat the heat with a few flaps.

WHAT YOU NEED

- A warm sidewalk
- Measuring cup (with ¼-cup marking or with metric measurements, if needed)
- Water
- Chalk
- Paper fan

WHAT YOU DO

STEP 1:

On a hot, sunny day, find a spot on a warm sidewalk where you can do your experiment and not be disturbed.

STEP 2:

Make two small puddles, each with 1¼ cups (60 mL) of water, about 3 feet (0.9 m) apart on the sidewalk. Wait for the water to settle, then draw a chalk outline around each puddle.

STEP 3:

Leave one puddle alone but fan the other puddle with your paper fan. Does it evaporate faster? Now feel the pavement. Is it cooler?

WHAT'S GOING ON?

When bees bring water into the nest and fan it, the water evaporates more quickly and cools the nest. This is exactly what you did. The flapping of your fan made the water molecules evaporate and cooled the sidewalk more quickly.

Read My Hips

When a forager scout finds a great patch of flowers with lots of pollen and great-tasting nectar, she rushes back home to tell the colony. But once she gets there, how does she describe where to find the treasure? Interpretive dance!

There are two kinds of dances bees perform. One is called the round dance. It shows other bees where nearby flowers are located. The scout moves in a circle and buzzes, calling attention to herself. The more she buzzes, the bigger the food source. Other bees approach and smell the scent of the flower. This provides enough information for them to discover the nearby source. They come back to the hive and dance. The bigger the dance party, the better the patch of flowers.

For more complicated directions, a bee does a waggle dance based on a figure eight. The bee moves in a direction, waggles, turns around, loops back, and waggles in the same direction as the first waggle.

The waggle dance tells other bees three things. First is the kind of flower the scout has found, which is obvious from the scent she has brought back with her. Second is the direction of the flower in relation to the sun, which she expresses with the angle in which she waggles. If she moves straight up, the flower is in the direction of the sun. Straight down, away from the sun. Left, to left of the sun. Right, to the right of sun. Third is the distance of the flower, which is expressed in the amount of shaking. More wiggle and jiggle means the patch is farther away. Less means the patch is nearby. The movements are amazingly precise. A half second of waggle represents about ⅓ of a mile (0.5 km) of flight distance away.

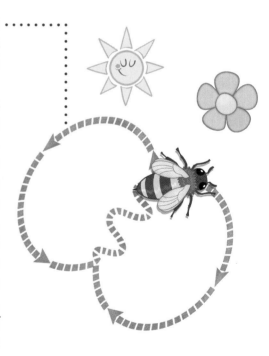

After the dance, forager bees take off and find the flower patch. They gather pollen and nectar and come back. After transferring their load, they do the same waggle dance to spread the word.

ACTIVITY:
Dances with Bees

Here's a game to really get your waggle on! Dance like a bee and see if you can "tell" people where the flower is hidden.

WHAT YOU NEED

- Chalk
- Pavement in a safe place to play
- At least two players
- A "flower" or anything that can stand in for a flower like a ball or a sock

WHAT YOU DO

STEP 1:

Set up the game.

- Draw a big circle, at least 6 to 7 feet (1.8 to 2.1 m) in diameter, with the chalk on the pavement. This is the hive.
- Draw a second circle inside the large one, about the size of a hula hoop. This is the compass that the scout bee uses for directions. Imagine the compass circle is like the face of a clock:
  - Draw a SUN at noon.
  - Put an E mark at 3 o'clock to represent EAST.
  - Put an S mark at 6 o'clock to represent SOUTH.
  - Put a W mark at 9 o'clock to represent WEST.

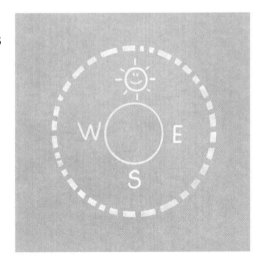

STEP 2:

Play.

- Choose a scout bee.
- All the other bees wait in the hive and close their eyes.
- The scout bee hides the flower where no one can see it.
- The bees open their eyes.
- The scout bee does a waggle dance on the compass to show the bees which direction the flower is in relation to the sun.
    - Waggle and walk in the direction of where the flower is hidden.
    - When you reach the edge of the compass, take a right turn and come back to the place you started and do the dance again.
    - At the end of that waggle take a left and return to the spot where you started.
    - The speed of the waggle says something about the distance from the "hive." A fast waggle means the flower is farther away. A slow waggle means it is nearby.
    - The bees look for the flower.
    - The bee that finds the flower becomes the scout bee.

Making Scents

Honeybees are great communicators. Not only do they dance to give directions, but they release strong-smelling scents to tell each other things, from "The queen is fine!" to "Something is attacking our nest!" to "This looks like a nice new home." Chemical signals work well in a nest. A scent is released into the air for all the bees to smell at the same time. It's like a big chemical billboard or internet post.

Hey, Honey, Do You Know What You're Eating?

Who doesn't love honey? Hope you still do once you know how it's made!

First, a forager bee lands on a flower and scoops the pollen into the basketlike sacks on her legs. Then she pokes her long, hollow tongue deep into the flower until she finds nectar. She sucks up the nectar and swallows it. It is stored in her special honey stomach, called a crop. A chemical in the crop breaks down the nectar into two main building-block sugars.

After she has visited and harvested about 100 flowers, the forager bee heads back to the nest with her baskets full of pollen and belly full of nectar. When she arrives, she is met by a nest bee, who greets her with an open mouth. The forager bee spits up the nectar from her crop into the mouth of the nest bee. The nest bee then squeezes the water out of the nectar by chewing it and spits the concentrated sugar syrup into a honeycomb cell for storage. When the honey is the right consistency, the worker puts a wax cap on it and keeps it in the cell to eat later on.

Why Does Honey Crystallize?

Honey is mostly made up of water and sugar. When there is a lot of sugar and not as much water, the sugar forms crystals. In organic honey, bits of wax and pollen can become a base for crystals to form on. That's why raw honey, which is usually unheated and less filtered than commercial honey, is more likely to crystallize. When stored in clean glass containers without exposure to air, and at a temperature of at least 77°F (25°C), crystals don't form as quickly. If honey is processed, heated, and filtered a lot, crystals are less likely to ever form. If it does crystallize, no problem. Let the closed jar of honey sit in a bath of warm water. The honey will warm up and the crystals will dissolve back into the solution.

Honey Is Hard Work

It takes a lot of work to be so sweet. Each worker bee, as soon as it graduates to work outside the nest, gathers nectar and pollen almost every day of its life and ends up making only about 1½ teaspoons (354.9 mL) of honey before it dies. A 1-pound (0.5 kg) jar of honey is the lifetime work of approximately 768 bees.

· = 6 bees

1-Pound Jar of Honey =

Healing Honey

Can honey keep things healthy? See what happens when you soak one apple slice in honey compared with leaving one out in the air.

WHAT YOU NEED

- Grown-up to help
- Apple
- Knife
- Three small dishes
- Honey (organic, if possible)
- Water

WHAT YOU DO

STEP 1:

Have your grown-up help you slice the apple into three equal pieces. Place one slice in each of the three dishes.

STEP 2:

Leave one slice alone. Cover the next slice with honey. Cover the last slice with water.

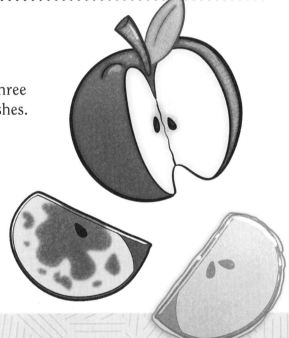

STEP 3:

Wait and watch.
Over the next few days, what do you notice?

WHAT'S GOING ON?

Honey has antimicrobial properties—that means it kills off microscopic bugs that can infect and decompose the apple. It has so much sugar content and so little water that microorganisms just can't survive in it. And without microorganisms, things don't rot. This is why honey is a great preservative. It likely could be stored forever if its container is airtight and kept in a cool area.

Security Strategies

There's treasure within the cells of a honeybee nest, and every bee that lives there knows it. Each worker is equipped and wired to defend the honey, larvae, and queen. And there's a lot to watch out for: bacterial infections, viruses, mites, fungi, mold, and other insects, not to mention birds, bears, and even humans. No matter what, bees are prepared for the worst and have a number of defenses to keep their home and family safe.

Tiny Terrors

Microorganisms or microbes are creatures that are way too small to see with the human eye. They include bacteria, fungi, viruses, and molds. These organisms are all around us all the time, but if they get too plentiful they can cause disease. Bees have a strategy to defend against microorganisms. Even before their nest is completely built, they smear the insides with propolis, a chewed-up mash of bee saliva, pollen, honey, beeswax, and bits of tree sap, buds, and bark. The concoction creates a protective barrier that kills mold, fungi, and bacteria that might invade and infect the colony.

Trespassers Beware

For intruders that aren't microscopic, bees also have plans in place. Every bee in the colony has a similar scent. If an invader flies in to cause trouble, the guard bees can smell the difference and get rid of the trespasser with a quick sting.

The Sting Is the Thing

Honeybees have a nasty sting. A sharp stinger is jammed into the skin of an intruder, followed by a jolt of venom squirted into the wound. The chemicals that make up bee venom cause itchiness and increased blood flow. This isn't accidental. Itching, rubbing, and increased heart rate make the venom flow to the rest of the body faster.

There has to be a real threat for the worker bee to unleash her poison. The stinger is barbed and gets stuck in the skin. When the bee flies away, she tears the tip of her abdomen off and dies.

Hot Ball

Another way to destroy an intruder is by getting hot and bothered. Literally. When a guard bee is alarmed and ready for a fight, she can heat up her belly to 100°F (37.8°C) by tensing and flexing her muscles. Wasps or other small pillaging insects can't live at temperatures so high. A group of bees swarms the wasp and surrounds it, heating it up until it's history. This is called thermoballing.

Crowd Control

If the threat is a big one, from a large animal that may devastate the colony, the bees send out a chemical alarm to their nestmates. This distress signal whips all the workers into a frenzy and they cloud together to form a massive coordinated attack on the intruder.

The thing to remember is that bees aren't out to kill. Venom is meant to cause pain, not death. They just want to protect their nest and to teach anything that disturbs them a lesson: "DON'T BUG OUR HOME!"

Honeybee Keeping

Humans have been keeping bees in man-made beehives since ancient times. People would trap swarms of wild bees in baskets, hollow logs, or clay containers. The bees would construct their honeycombs in the containers and people would harvest the honey.

Modern wood-frame beehives showed up in the 1800s. Frames are hung down from a main structure and bees create their honeycombs within the frames in the brood chamber. Bees enter from the bottom. Some beekeepers use a queen excluder, which makes it impossible for the large queens to pass through the brood chamber. This keeps the queen in a certain area and allows smaller worker bees to pass through and store honey in the additional super units. The vertical frames can be easily removed for honey harvesting and replaced for new growth.

Dress for Success

Beekeepers have special suits and helmets with mesh front panels. These suits and helmets cover every single inch of the keeper. Keepers also use smoke cans. The smoke causes the bees to slurp up honey quickly and makes them sluggish. Sluggish, full-bellied bees are less likely to sting. Other hive tools include flattened pieces of steel used to scrape, pry, or separate frames that get stuck together with honey.

Smoke Can

Honey Frame
hangs inside Brood Chamber

Cover

Honey Super

Queen Excluder

Brood Chamber

Bottom Board
Stand

RESOURCES

ONLINE INFORMATION

USDA Bee Research Laboratory:

ars.usda.gov/northeast-area/beltsville-md/beltsville-agricultural-research-center/bee-research-laboratory

The Xerces Society Native Bee Biology:

xerces.org/pollinator-conservation/native-bees

The British Royal Entomological Society:

royensoc.co.uk

The Honeybee Conservancy—Mason Bees:

thehoneybeeconservancy.org/mason-bees

USDA-ARS-PWA Pollinating Insect Research Unit:

ars.usda.gov/pacific-west-area/logan-ut/pollinating-insect-biology-management-systematics-research

(check out the research pages for added information about the native bees in the U.S.)

The American Beekeeping Federation:

abfnet.org

The Pollinator Partnership and associated North American Pollinator Protection Campaign:

pollinator.org

MASON BEE SUPPLIES

Crown Bees: crownbees.com

Mason Bees for Sale: masonbeesforsale.com

ACKNOWLEDGMENTS

A book like this doesn't just happen on its own. There is so much thinking and bouncing off, research and development, tweaking and polishing, and creativity from a number of different sources that go into it from the moment the idea sparks until the day the book is released into the wild. It's truly a group effort. With that in mind, I would like to thank a handful of folks.

On the pondering level, I need to thank my creative and go-to queen bees and word-smithies: Dinah Manoff, Suzanne Selfors, Susan Wiggs, Laurie Frankel, Deb Caletti, Carol Cassella, Meg Parsont, Amy Johnson, Maryjane Johnston, Raquel Jaramillo, Jill Beermann, Debbie Gray, Mary Cushman, Megan Drew, Warren Read, Maura Conron, Wendy Orville, Trang Carola, and Maria Carola.

I couldn't have done it without my green-thumbers: Cindy Hennessey, Sabina Hammel, Kathy Glanzrock, Toshi Takeno, Susan Rutledge, Colleen Uyekawa, Liz Cooper, and Robin Hansen.

Thanks to my sweet dad, Jim Brunelle, whom I depend on for copyediting and idea shaping.

Thanks to my big brother, Bill Brunelle, who was there with me each and every one of the eight times I was stung by a bee as a kid. Now I know they sure weren't mason bees!

Thanks to all the wonderful people at Workman, and especially Daniel Nayeri and Suzie Bolotin for seeing the potential. Thanks to my amazing editor, Justin Krasner, for his vision, insight, and humor. Thanks to Carolyn Bahar, Amanda Hong, Colleen AF Venable, Doug Wolff, and the publicity, marketing, and sales teams.

Special thanks to Anna-Maria Jung for her sweet, sassy, and fun illustrations.

A huge thanks to Diana Cox-Foster of the USDA Bee Lab for making sure all the bee science was right.

And finally a shout-out to the bee testers, supporters, and observers at the heart of my hive: Keith, Kai, and Leo.

ROOMS WITH A VIEW

The following pages can be torn out of the book and rolled into inviting nesting tubes for a solitary bee to call home. Wrap each page around a pencil and tape it so it won't unroll. See pages 50–52 for directions on how to turn this book into a beehive!

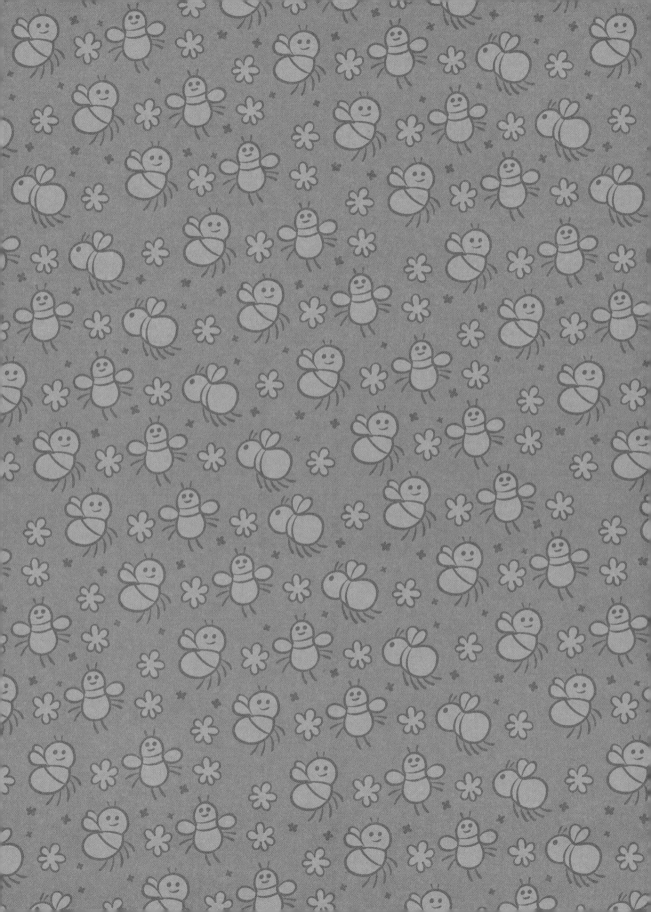

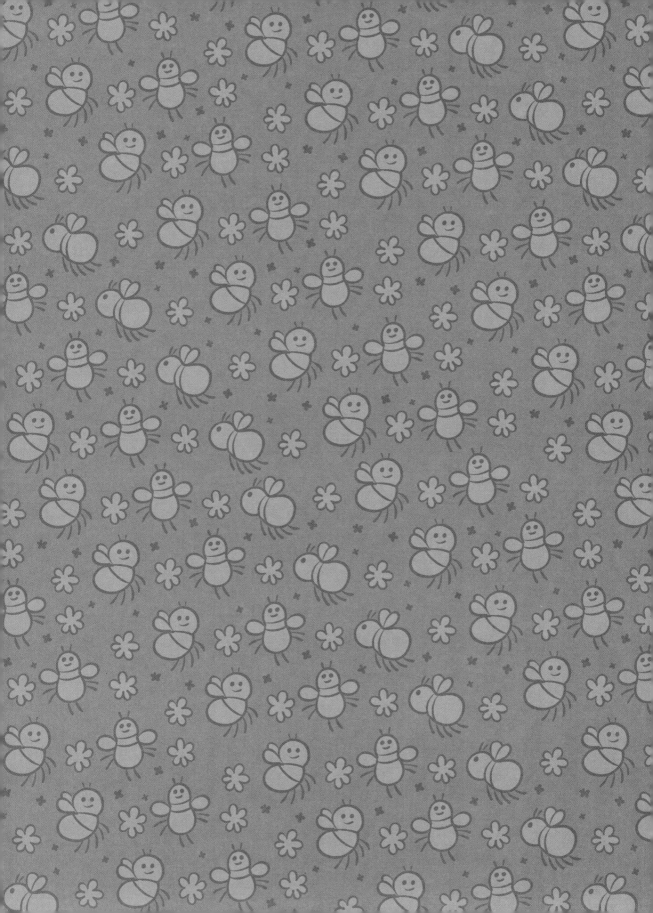

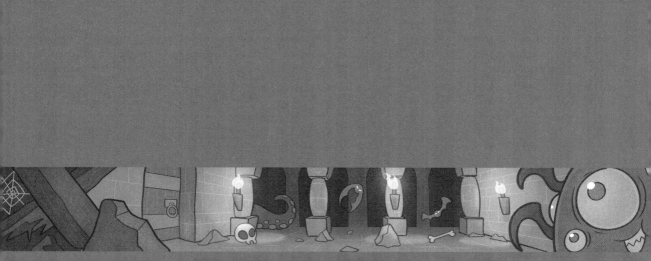

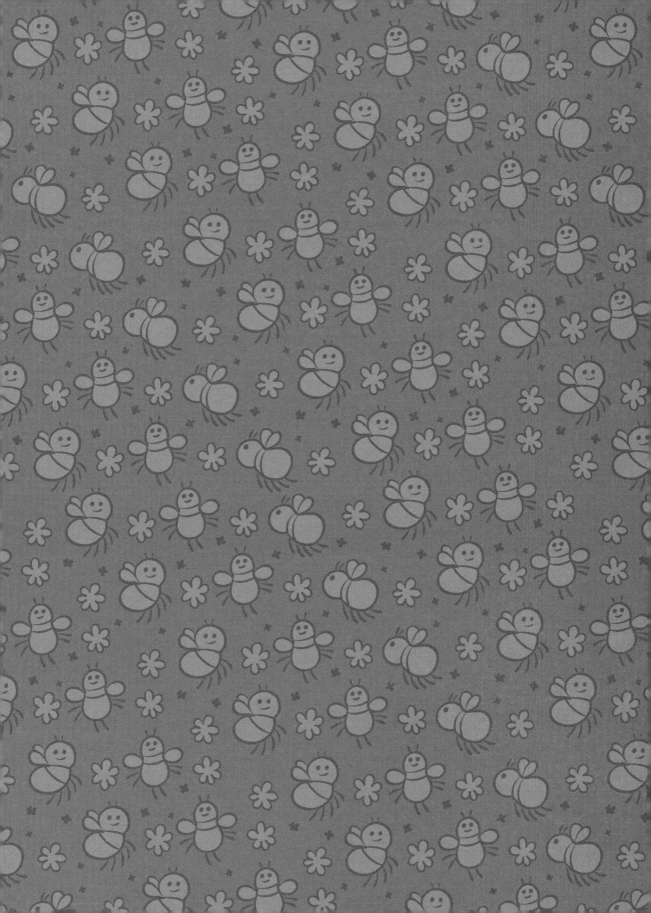

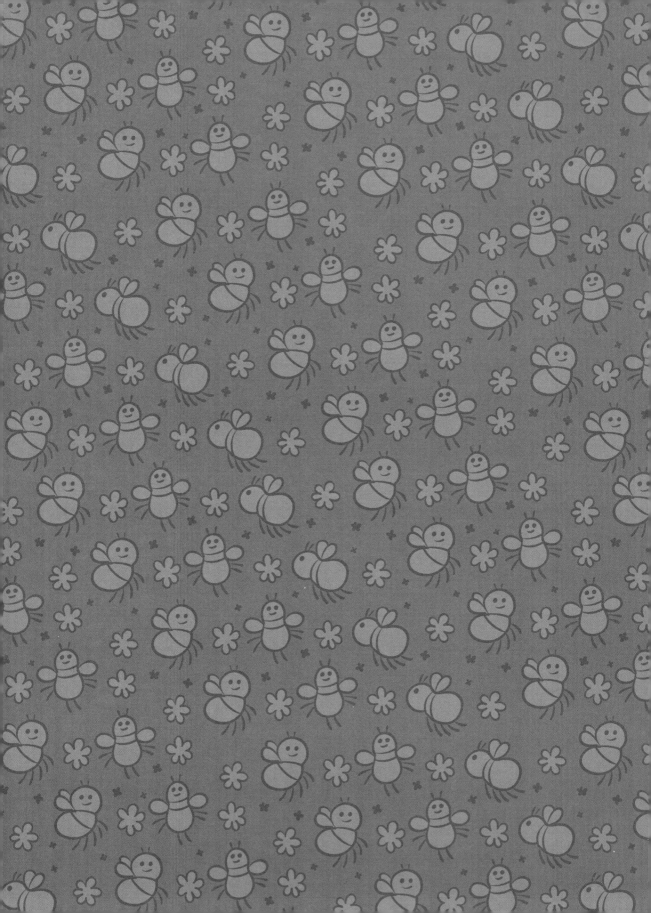

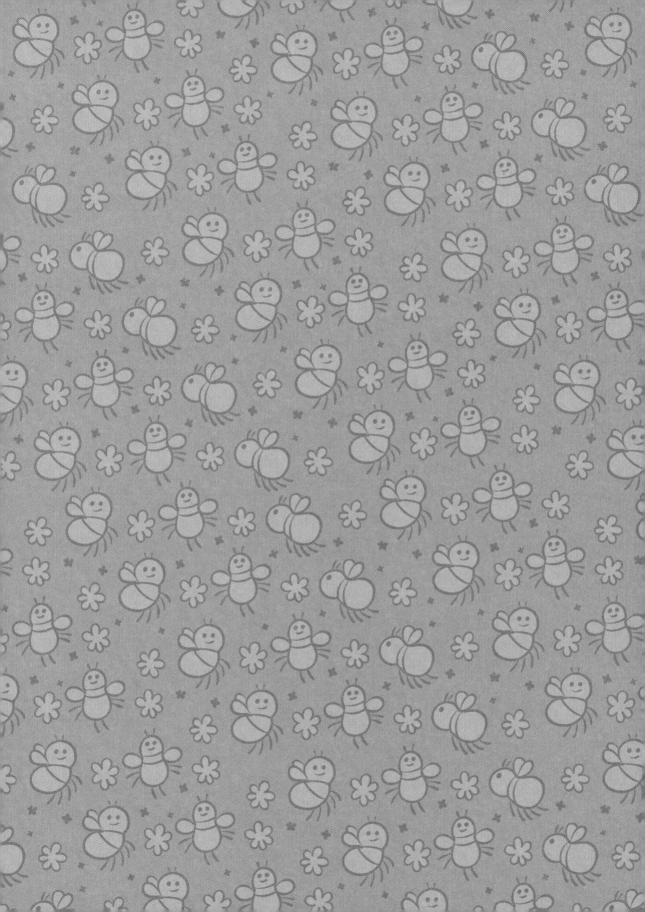

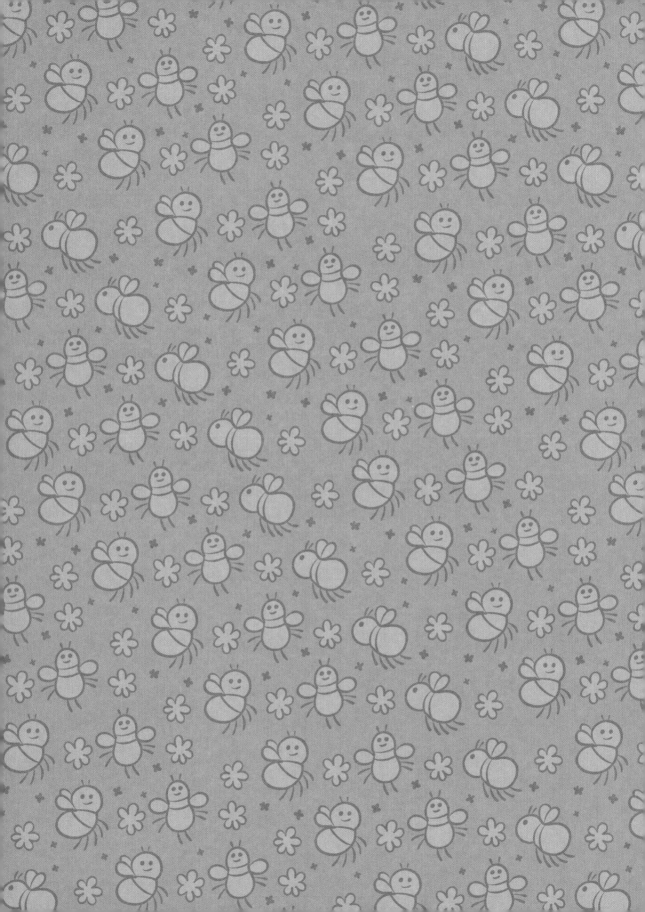

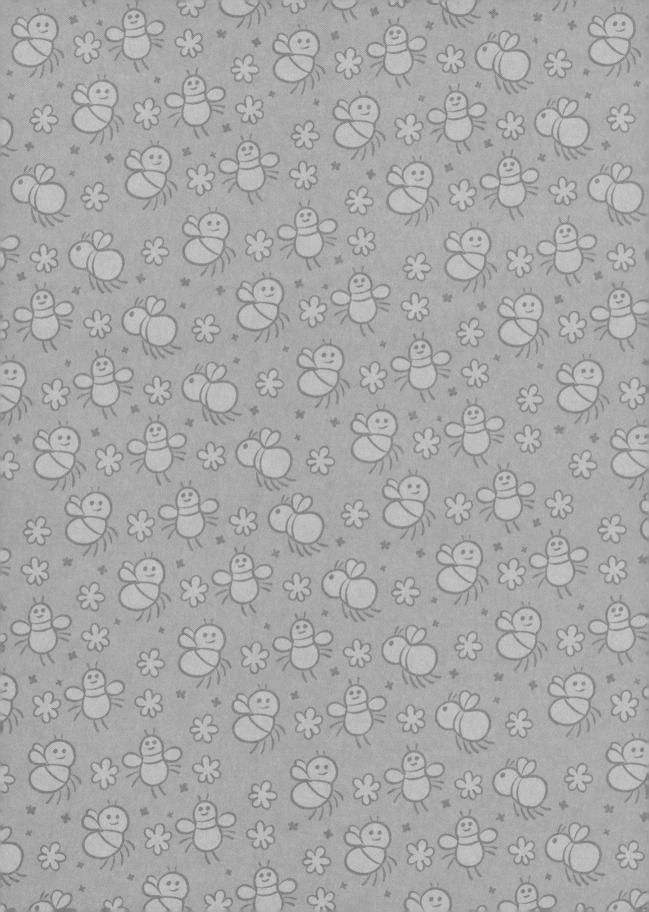

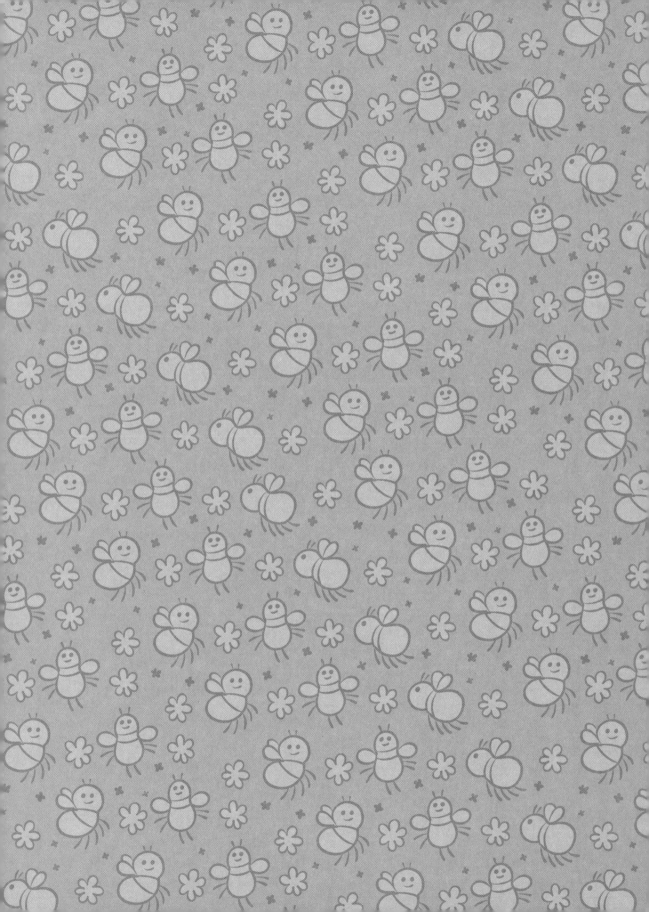

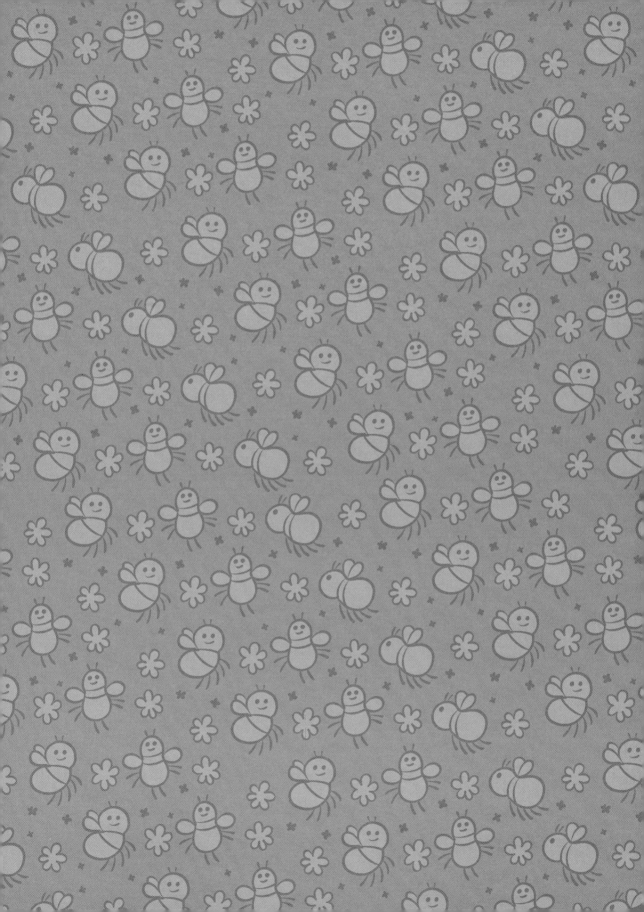

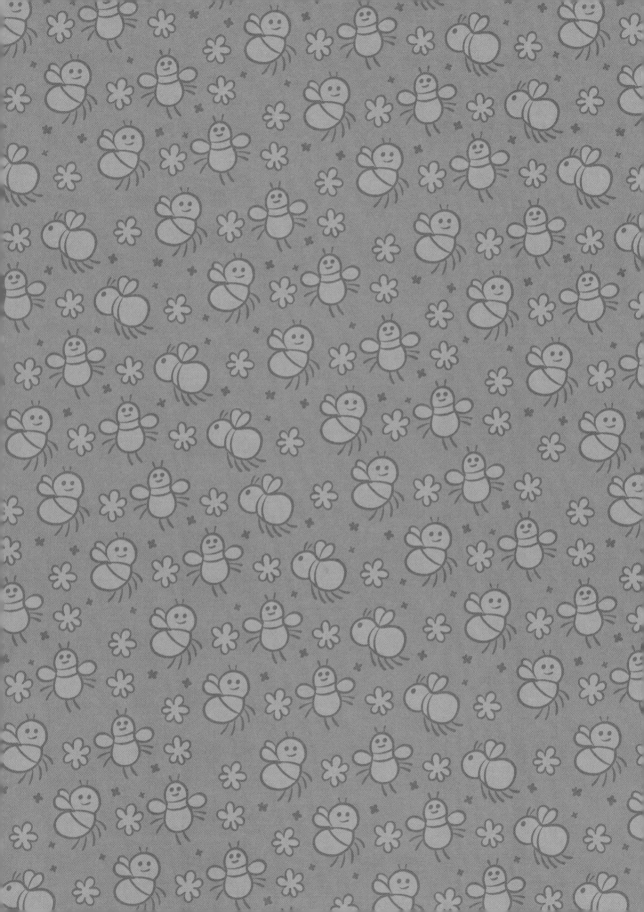

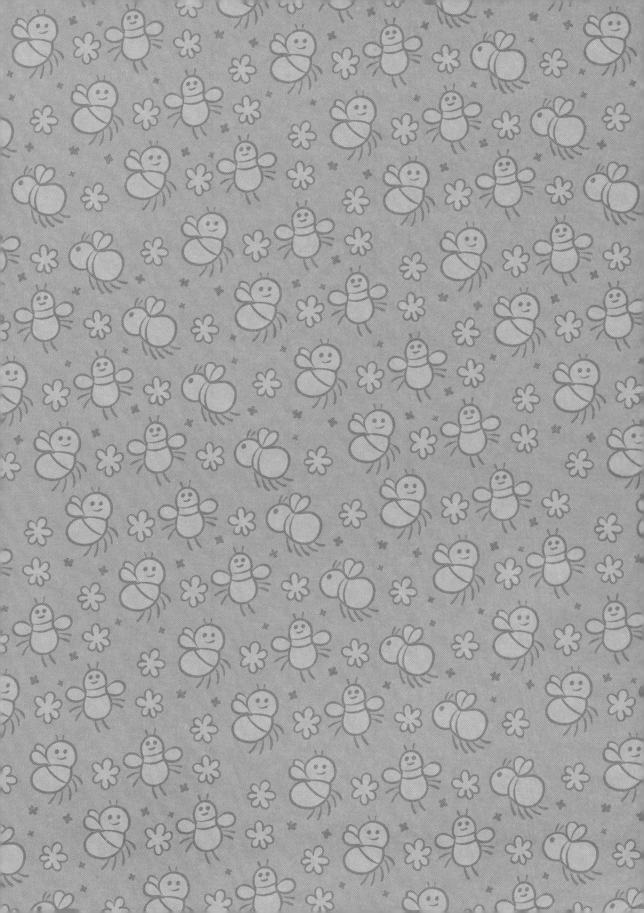

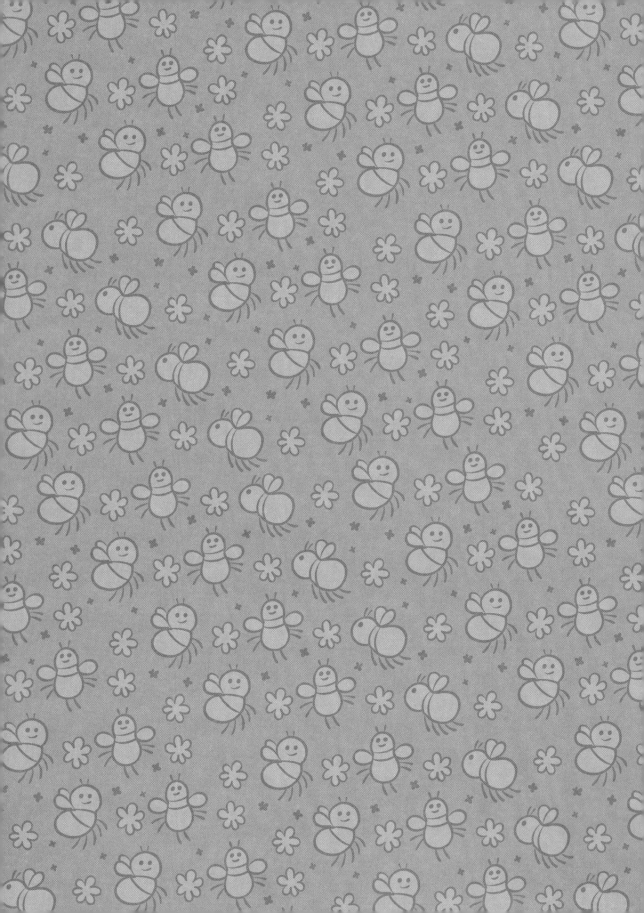

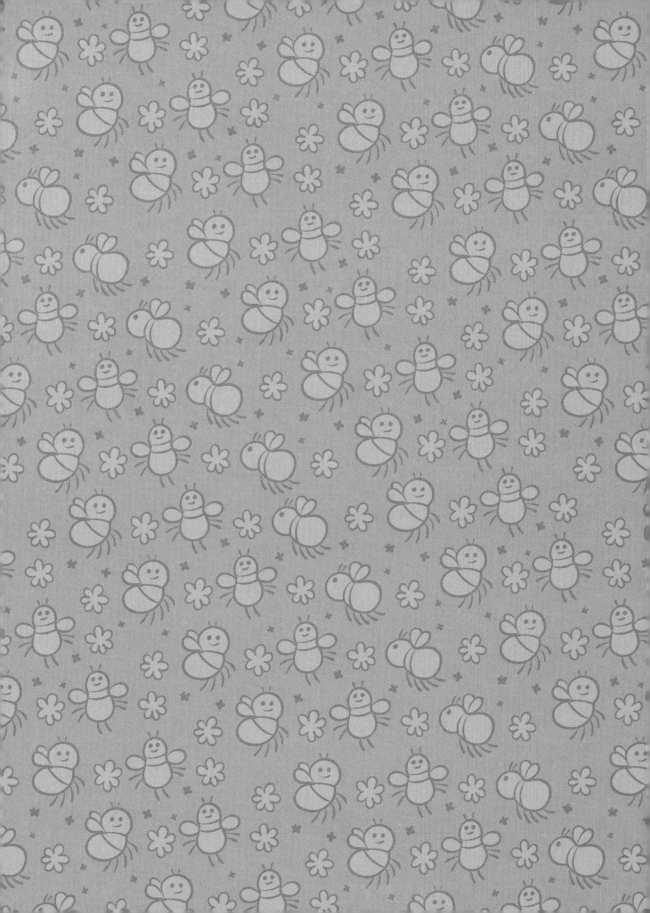

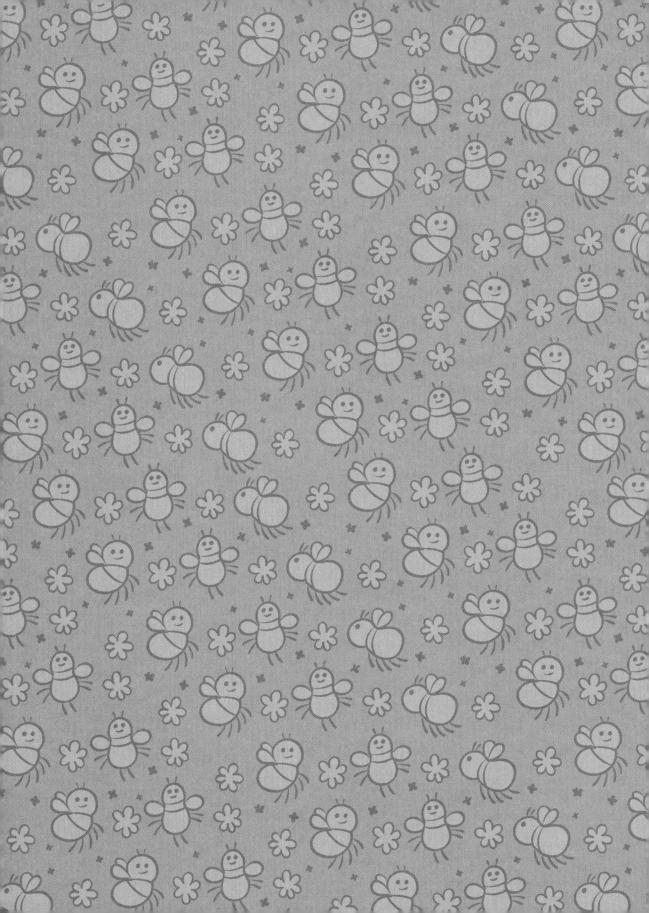

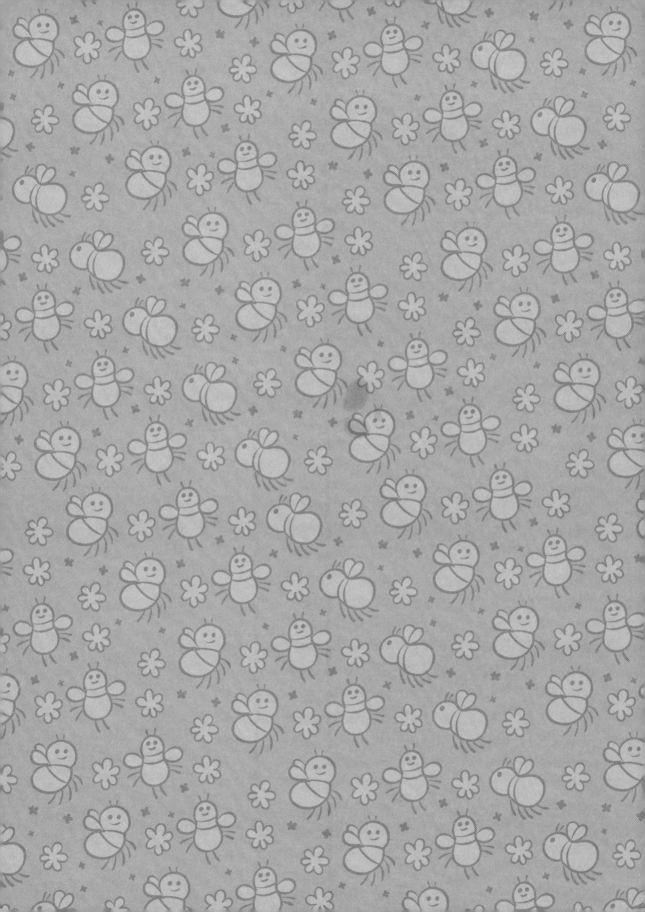

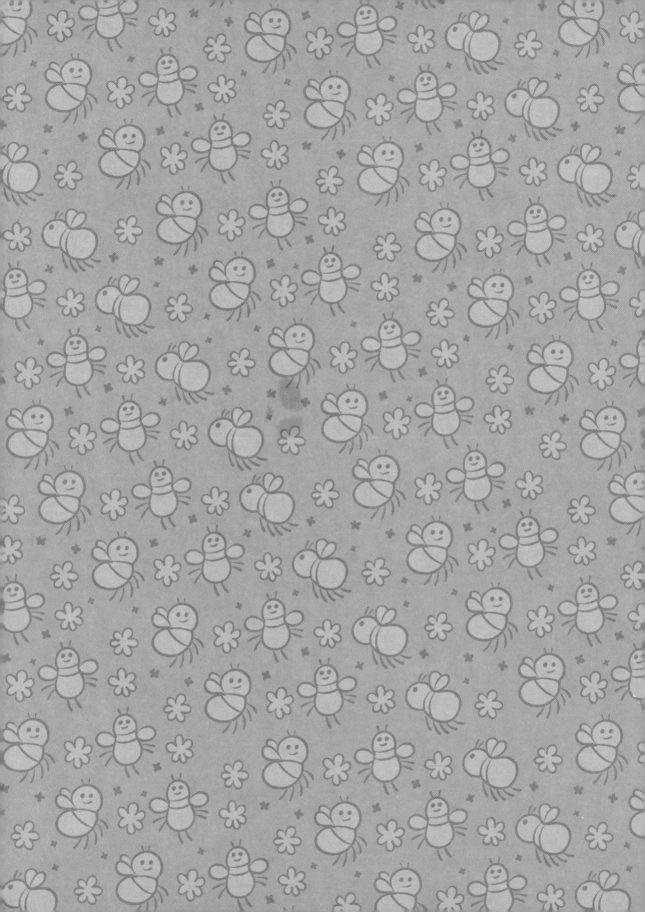